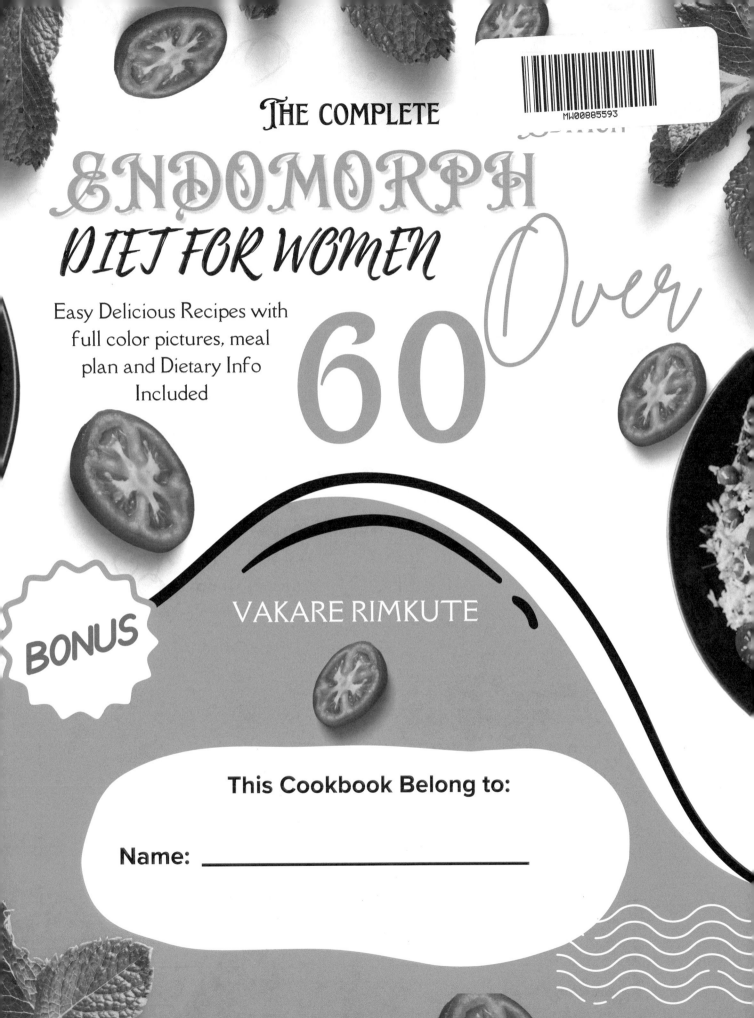

THE COMPLETE

ENDOMORPH

DIET FOR WOMEN

Easy Delicious Recipes with full color pictures, meal plan and Dietary Info Included

Over 60

BONUS

VAKARE RIMKUTE

This Cookbook Belong to:

Name: _____

Introduction to Endomorph Deit

Welcome to "Nourish: An Endomorph Diet Cookbook for Women Over 60." In the pages that follow, you will embark on a culinary journey designed to nourish your body, delight your taste buds, and support your journey to optimal health and vitality.

Embracing Your Unique Journey

As a woman over 60, you understand the importance of taking care of yourself and prioritizing your health. But with so much information out there, finding the right approach to nutrition can feel overwhelming. That's where this cookbook comes in.

Understanding Your Endomorph Body

If you're an endomorph, you know that your body has its own unique set of needs and challenges. With a tendency to hold onto weight more easily, finding the right balance of nutrients is crucial. This cookbook is tailored specifically to support the needs of endomorphs, providing you with recipes that are both delicious and nutritionally balanced.

The Power of Food

Food is more than just fuel—it's medicine. By nourishing your body with wholesome, nutrient-dense ingredients, you can support your overall health and well-being. From vibrant fruits and vegetables to lean proteins and healthy fats, every recipe in this cookbook is thoughtfully crafted to provide you with the nutrients you need to thrive.

Get ready to embark on a culinary adventure like no other. Whether you're a seasoned chef or a novice in the kitchen, you'll find recipes here that will inspire and delight you. From hearty soups and salads to decadent desserts and everything in between, there's something for everyone to enjoy.

But this cookbook is more than just a collection of recipes —it's a community. Join us as we come together to support each other on our journey to better health. Share your successes, swap tips and tricks, and celebrate the joys of nourishing your body from the inside out.

So here's to you, dear reader. Here's to embracing your unique journey, nourishing your body with love and intention, and living your best life at any age. Let this cookbook be your guide as you embark on a journey to better health and vitality.

Let's get cooking!

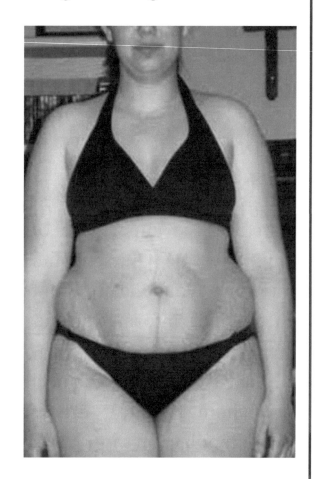

TABLE OF Content

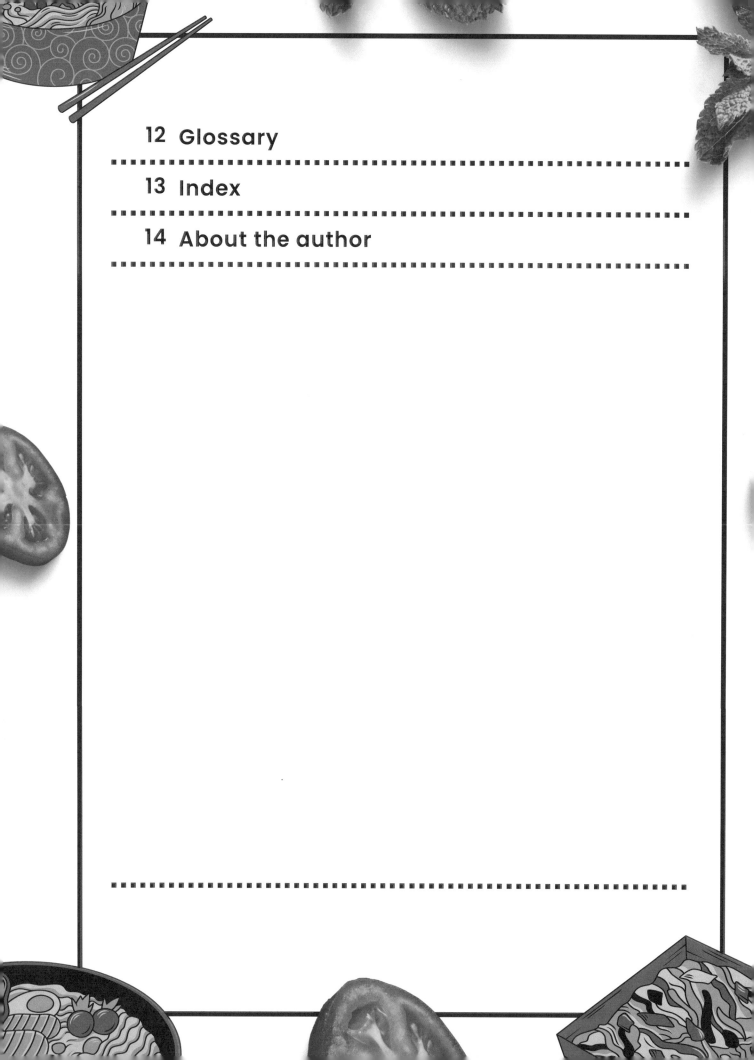

The Endomorph Diet Basic

What is an Endomorph?

• • •

An endomorph is one of the three primary somatotypes, or body types, classified by American psychologist William Sheldon in the 1940s. Individuals with an endomorphic body type tend to have certain physical characteristics and metabolic traits that distinguish them from the other somatotypes, which are ectomorph and mesomorph.

Physical Characteristics

- **Higher Body Fat Percentage:** Endomorphs generally have a higher proportion of body fat compared to muscle.
- **Rounder and Softer Body:** Their bodies tend to be round and soft, often with a wider waist and hips.
- **Shorter Limbs:** They typically have shorter limbs and a more compact bone structure.
- **Wide Hips and Shoulders:** Endomorphs often have a wide waist and broad shoulders, giving them a stocky appearance.

Types of Endomorph

1. **Pure Endomorph**
Characteristics:
- Displays the classic endomorph traits most prominently.
- Higher body fat percentage, particularly around the abdomen, hips, and thighs.
- A rounder, softer body shape with a larger bone structure.
- Slow metabolism, making it easier to gain weight and harder to lose it.

2. **Endo-Mesomorph**
Characteristics:
- Combination of endomorphic and mesomorphic traits.
- Possesses a muscular build but with a higher tendency to gain fat.
- Easier time building muscle compared to a pure endomorph.
- Still needs to manage diet carefully to avoid excessive fat gain.

Example: A person who can gain muscle relatively easily but also tends to gain fat quickly if not careful with diet and exercise.

2

Type of Endomorph?

3. Endo-Ectomorph

Characteristics:

- Combination of endomorphic and ectomorphic traits.
- Leaner limbs compared to pure endomorphs but retains a higher body fat percentage, particularly in the midsection.
- May have a slightly faster metabolism than a pure endomorph but still prone to weight gain.

Example: A person with a slimmer upper body and limbs but carries more weight around the waist and hips.

4. Metabolically Obese Normal Weight (MONW) Endomorph

Characteristics:

- Appears to have a normal weight based on BMI but carries a higher percentage of body fat.
- Fat is often distributed around the midsection.
- May exhibit signs of metabolic syndrome such as insulin resistance, high blood pressure, and dyslipidemia.
- Example: An individual who looks slim but has a high body fat percentage and potential metabolic health issues.

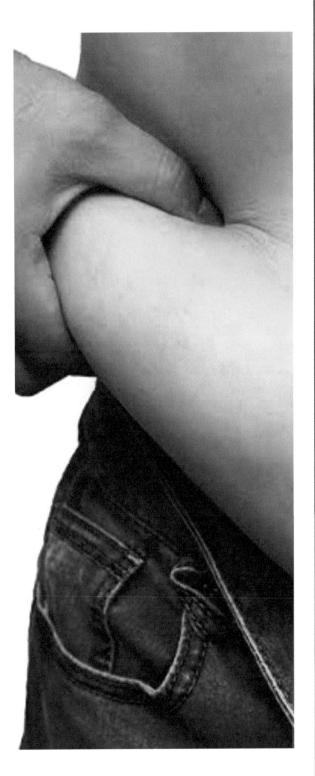

Dietary Needs of Endomorphs

Macronutrient Balance

1. Protein
- Importance: Protein is crucial for muscle maintenance, repair, and growth, especially as muscle mass tends to decline with age.
- Sources: Lean meats (chicken, turkey, lean cuts of beef), fish, eggs, dairy products (Greek yogurt, cottage cheese), legumes, and plant-based proteins (tofu, tempeh).

2. Carbohydrates
- Importance: Carbohydrates provide energy, but endomorphs should focus on complex carbohydrates that are digested slowly.
- Sources: Whole grains (quinoa, brown rice, oats), vegetables (especially non-starchy ones like leafy greens, broccoli, cauliflower), fruits (berries, apples, pears), and legumes.

3. Fats
- Importance: Healthy fats are essential for hormone production, brain health, and satiety.
- Sources: Avocado, nuts and seeds, olive oil, fatty fish (salmon, mackerel), and nut butters.

Caloric Intake
- **Moderate Caloric Deficit**: To facilitate weight loss or maintenance, a moderate caloric deficit may be necessary. This should be achieved by reducing calorie intake slightly while increasing physical activity, rather than through drastic calorie cuts which can slow metabolism further.
- **Portion Control**: Monitoring portion sizes to avoid overeating, even of healthy foods, is important. Smaller, more frequent meals can help regulate appetite and blood sugar levels.

4

Dietary Needs of Endomorphs

Meal Timing

- **Frequent, Balanced Meals:** Eating smaller, balanced meals every 3-4 hours can help keep metabolism active and prevent overeating.
- Avoiding Late-Night Eating: Consuming most calories earlier in the day and avoiding heavy meals late at night can improve digestion and support weight management.

Hydration

- **Importance**: Staying hydrated is crucial for metabolism, digestion, and overall health. Aim for at least 8-10 glasses of water per day.
- **Hydration Tips:** Drinking water before meals can help with portion control, and incorporating hydrating foods (like cucumbers, watermelon, and oranges) can contribute to overall hydration.

Micronutrient Needs

- **Calcium and Vitamin D:** Important for bone health, especially in postmenopausal women. Sources include dairy products, fortified plant milks, leafy greens, and exposure to sunlight.
- **B Vitamins**: Essential for energy metabolism. Sources include whole grains, lean meats, dairy products, eggs, and leafy greens.
- **Magnesium**: Supports muscle function and metabolic health. Sources include nuts, seeds, leafy greens, and whole grains.
- **Omega-3 Fatty Acids**: Anti-inflammatory benefits and support for heart health. Sources include fatty fish, flaxseeds, chia seeds, and walnuts.

Fiber intake

- **Importance**: Fiber aids in digestion, helps regulate blood sugar levels, and promotes satiety.
- **Sources**: Whole grains, fruits, vegetables, legumes, nuts, and seeds.

Special Considerations for Women Over 60

Hormonal Changes

- **Menopause and Estrogen Decline:** The decrease in estrogen levels during menopause can lead to weight gain, especially around the abdomen. Phytoestrogens, found in foods like soy products, flaxseeds, and legumes, can help balance hormone levels.

- **Bone Health:** The risk of osteoporosis increases post-menopause. Ensuring adequate intake of calcium and vitamin D is crucial for maintaining bone density. Sources include dairy products, fortified plant milks, leafy greens, and supplements if necessary.

- **Hot Flashes and Night Sweats:** Certain foods may help manage these symptoms, such as those rich in omega-3 fatty acids (salmon, flaxseeds) and avoiding triggers like caffeine and spicy foods.

Metabolism & Weight Management

- **weight**. A diet high in protein and fiber can help boost metabolism and promote satiety.

- **Portion Control and Caloric Needs:** Caloric needs typically decrease with age. Focusing on nutrient-dense foods and practicing portion control is essential. Smaller, frequent meals can help manage hunger and energy levels.

Heart Health

- **Cardiovascular Risk:** Post-menopausal women have a higher risk of heart disease. Emphasizing heart-healthy fats (like those from avocados, nuts, and olive oil) and reducing saturated fats and cholesterol is important.

- **Fiber and Cholesterol:** High-fiber diets can help manage cholesterol levels. Include plenty of whole grains, fruits, vegetables, and legumes.

Muscle Mass and Strength

- **Muscle Loss (Sarcopenia):** Age-related muscle loss can affect metabolism and physical function. Adequate protein intake (lean meats, fish, dairy, legumes) and strength training exercises can help preserve muscle mass.
- **Protein Distribution:** Spreading protein intake throughout the day supports muscle protein synthesis. Aim for balanced protein in each meal.

Hydration and Digestion

- **Hydration Needs:** As the body ages, the sense of thirst may diminish. Ensure regular fluid intake through water, herbal teas, and hydrating foods like cucumbers and watermelon.
- **Digestive Health:** Aging can slow down digestion. A diet high in fiber (whole grains, fruits, vegetables) and staying hydrated can help maintain regularity and digestive health.

Micronutrient Requirements

- **Calcium and Vitamin D:** Essential for bone health. Sources include dairy, fortified plant milks, leafy greens, and safe sun exposure.
- **B Vitamins:** Important for energy metabolism and cognitive function. Sources include whole grains, lean meats, dairy, eggs, and leafy greens.
- **Magnesium:** Supports muscle and nerve function. Found in nuts, seeds, whole grains, and leafy greens.
- **Iron:** While post-menopausal women may need less iron, it's still important to include iron-rich foods like lean meats, legumes, and fortified cereals to prevent anemia.

Cognitive Health

- **Omega-3 Fatty Acids:** Beneficial for brain health. Include sources like fatty fish (salmon, mackerel), flaxseeds, chia seeds, and walnuts.
- **Antioxidant-Rich Foods:** Protect against cognitive decline. Berries, dark leafy greens, nuts, and seeds are excellent choices.

Understanding Ingredients

Reading Labels

- **Serving Sizes**: Pay attention to serving sizes to understand the nutritional content.
- **Calories**: Monitor calorie intake to maintain a balanced diet.
- **Fats**: Look for healthy fats and avoid trans fats and high levels of saturated fats.
- **Sodium**: Choose products with lower sodium content to maintain heart health.
- **Added Sugars**: Minimize products with high added sugar content.
- **Ingredients List**: Opt for products with simple, whole ingredients and avoid those with long lists of unfamiliar additives.

Buying Organic vs. Conventional

- **Prioritize Organic**: For produce like strawberries, spinach, and apples, which often have higher pesticide levels.
- **Conventional Produce**: Safer options include avocados, sweet corn, and pineapples, which have lower pesticide residues.

Choosing Fresh Produce

- **Seasonal Fruits and Vegetables**: Select in-season produce for better flavor, nutrition, and cost-effectiveness.
- **Variety of Colors**: Incorporate a rainbow of fruits and vegetables to ensure a wide range of nutrients.
- **Organic Options:** Consider organic options for produce with high pesticide residues (refer to the "Dirty Dozen" list).

Meal Prep Ingredients

- **Pre-washed Greens**: For quick salads and smoothies.
- **Pre-cut Vegetables**: Saves time in meal prep and encourages healthy eating.
- **Cooked Grains**: Prepare in bulk and store for use throughout the week.
- **Roasted Chicken or Turkey**: Ready-to-use proteins for salads, sandwiches, and main dishes.

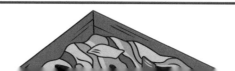

COOKING TOOLS

ESSENTIAL KNIVES

Egg Sandwich Bites

Sausage Munchers

Tuna Tartare

Fresh Salmon Sashimi

Rockefeller Oysters

Fresh Spring Rolls

Friend Fish Sticks

CUTTING BOARDS

Wooden Cutting Boards

Plastic Cutting Boards

Flexible Cutting Mats

MEASURING TOOLS

Measuring Cups (liquid and dry)

Measuring Spoons

UTENSILS

Spatulas (heat-resistant silicone)

Wooden Spoons

Tongs

Whisks

Ladles

MIXING BOWLS

Stainless Steel Bowls

Glass Bowls

Nesting Bowls

APPLIANCES

Blender

Food Processor

Slow Cooker

Instant Pot

Steamer

Digital Kitchen Scale

Essential Tools and Appliances

Whole Grains
- Quinoa
- Brown Rice
- Oats
- Whole Wheat Pasta

Proteins
- Lean Meats (chicken, turkey)
- Fish and Seafood
- Eggs
- Legumes (beans, lentils)
- Nuts and Seeds

Healthy Fats
- Olive Oil
- Avocado Oil
- Nuts and Nut Butters
- Chia Seeds
- Flaxseeds

Spices and Herbs
- Basil, Oregano, Thyme, Rosemary
- Cumin, Coriander, Turmeric, Paprika
- Salt and Pepper
- Garlic and Onion Powder

Condiments
- Low-Sodium Soy Sauce or Tamari
- Vinegars (apple cider, balsamic)
- Mustard
- Hot Sauce
- Salsa

Canned and Jarred Goods
- Tomatoes (diced, crushed, paste)
- Beans (black, chickpeas, kidney)
- Tuna or Salmon (packed in water)
- Vegetable Broth

Baking Essentials
- Whole Wheat Flour
- Almond Flour
- Baking Powder
- Baking Soda
- Honey
- Maple Syrup

Snacks
- Dried Fruits (without added sugar)
- Dark Chocolate (70% cocoa or higher)
- Rice Cakes

COMMON COOKING MEASUREMENTS

Volume Measurements

MEASUREMENT	EQUIVALENT
1 teaspoon (tsp)	1/3 tablespoon (tbsp)
1 teaspoon (tsp)	3 teaspoons (tsp)
1/8 cup	2 tablespoons (tbsp)
1/4 cup	4 tablespoons (tbsp)
1/3 cup	5 tablespoons + 1 teaspoon
1/2 cup	8 tablespoons (tbsp)
3/4 cup	12 tablespoons (tbsp)
1 cup	16 tablespoons (tbsp)
1 pint (pt)	2 cups
1 quart (qt)	4 cups
1 gallon (gal)	16 cups

COMMON COOKING MEASUREMENTS

Weight Measurements

MEASUREMENT	EQUIVALENT
1 ounce (oz)	28.35 grams (g)
1 pound (lb)	16 ounces (oz)
1 kilogram (kg)	2.2 pounds (lbs)

Liquid Measurements

MEASUREMENT	EQUIVALENT
1 fluid ounce (fl oz)	2 tablespoons (tbsp)
1 cup	8 fluid ounces (fl oz)
1 pint (pt)	16 fluid ounces (fl oz)
1 quart (qt)	32 fluid ounces (fl oz)
1 gallon (gal)	128 fluid ounces (fl oz)

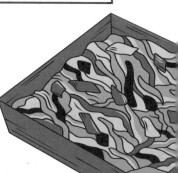

OVEN TEMPERATURES

Temperature Conversions

FAHRENHEIT (°F)	CELSIUS (°C)	GAS MARK
250°F	120°C	1/2
275°F	135°C	1
300°F	150°C	2
325°F	165°C	3
350°F	175°C	4
375°F	190°C	5
400°F	200°C	6
425°F	220°C	7
450°F	230°C	8
475°F	245°C	9
500°F	260°C	10

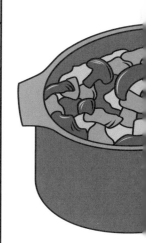

METRIC CONVERSIONS

Volume

METRIC	U.S. EQUIVALENT
1 milliliter (ml)	0.034 fluid ounces (fl oz)
100 milliliters	3.4 fluid ounces (fl oz)
1 liter (l)	34 fluid ounces (fl oz)
1 liter (l)	4.2 cups
1 liter (l)	2.1 pints

Weight

METRIC	U.S. EQUIVALENT
1 gram (g)	0.035 ounces (oz)
100 grams (g)	3.5 ounces (oz)
500 grams (g)	17.6 ounces (oz)
1 kilogram (kg)	2.2 pounds (lbs)

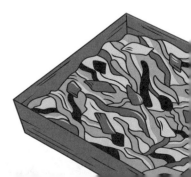

COMMON COOKING MEASUREMENTS

Volume Measurements

MEASUREMENT	EQUIVALENT
tsp	teaspoon
tbsp	tablespoon
Cup	Cup
oz	ounce
lb	pound
ml	milliliter
l	liter
g	gram
Kg	Kilogram
fl oz	fluid ounce

COMMON COOKING MEASUREMENTS

Volume Measurements

1 cup all-purpose flour = 120 grams
1 cup granulated sugar = 200 grams
1 cup brown sugar = 220 grams
1 cup butter = 227 grams (or 2 sticks)
1 large egg = 50 grams

Note:

- When measuring dry ingredients, use a spoon to fill the measuring cup or spoon, and level off with a flat edge for accuracy.
- For liquid ingredients, use a clear measuring cup and check at eye level.
- When converting recipes, be mindful of the precision required for baking versus cooking.

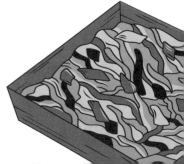

CHAPTER 1

BREAKFAST DELIGHTS

SHAKSHUKA WITH FRESH HERBS

Ingredients

- 1 tbsp olive oil
- 1 onion, chopped
- 2 cloves garlic, minced
- 1 red bell pepper, diced
- 1 yellow bell pepper, diced
- 1 tsp ground cumin
- 1 tsp paprika
- Salt and pepper to taste
- 1 can (14 oz) diced tomatoes
- 4 large eggs
- 2 tbsp fresh parsley, chopped
- 2 tbsp fresh cilantro, chopped

Instructions

- Heat olive oil in a large skillet over medium heat. Add chopped onion and cook until soft, about 3-4 minutes.
- Stir in minced garlic, diced red and yellow bell peppers, ground cumin, paprika, salt, and pepper. Cook for 5 more minutes until peppers are tender.
- Pour in diced tomatoes with their juices. Let it simmer for 10 minutes until slightly thickened.
- Using a spoon, make small wells in the tomato-pepper mixture. Crack one egg into each well.
- Cover the skillet and cook eggs for 5-7 minutes, until whites are set but yolks are runny.
- Sprinkle chopped parsley and cilantro over the top.
- Serve hot directly from the skillet. Optional: top with crumbled feta cheese and serve with crusty bread or pita.

Preparation Time : 10 min

Total Time : 30 min

Servings : 4

Nutritional Info

- Calories: 180
- Protein: 8g
- Carbohydrates: 10g
- Fat: 12g
- Fiber: 3g

OATMEAL WITH FRESH FRUIT AND NUTS

Ingredients

- 4 large egg whites
- 1 cup fresh spinach, chopped
- 1/2 cup cherry tomatoes, halved
- 1/4 cup onions, finely chopped
- 1 clove garlic, minced
- 1 tablespoon olive oil
- Salt and pepper, to taste

Instructions

- Chop the spinach, halve the tomatoes, finely chop the onions, and mince the garlic.
- Heat olive oil in a skillet over medium heat.
- Add onions and garlic, cook for 2-3 minutes until soft.
- Add spinach and tomatoes, cook for 2-3 minutes until spinach is wilted. Remove from skillet.
- Whisk egg whites with a pinch of salt and pepper.
- Pour into the skillet and cook for 2 minutes until edges start to set.
- Spoon the spinach and tomato mix onto one half of the omelet.
- Fold the omelet in half over the vegetables.
- Cook for another 2-3 minutes until fully set.
- Slide onto a plate, garnish with herbs if desired, and serve immediately.

 Preparation Time : 10 min

 Total Time : 20 min

Servings : 1

Nutritional Info

- Calories: 110
- Protein: 12g
- Carbohydrates: 5g
- Fat: 4g
- Fiber: 2g

SMOKED SALMON AND CUCUMBER SALAD

Ingredients

- 200g smoked salmon, sliced
- 1 English cucumber, thinly sliced
- 1/4 red onion, thinly sliced
- 2 tablespoons capers
- 2 tablespoons fresh dill, chopped
- 2 tablespoons olive oil
- 1 tablespoon lemon juice
- Salt and pepper to taste

Instructions

- In a large bowl, combine the sliced cucumber, red onion, capers, and chopped dill.
- In a small bowl, whisk together the olive oil and lemon juice to make the dressing. Season with salt and pepper to taste.
- Pour the dressing over the cucumber mixture and toss gently to coat.
- Arrange the smoked salmon slices on a serving platter.
- Spoon the cucumber salad over the smoked salmon slices.
- Garnish with extra dill if desired.
- Serve immediately and enjoy!

Preparation Time : 10 min

Total Time : 0 min

Servings : 4

Nutritional Info

- Calories: 150 kcal
- Protein: 12g
- Fat: 8g
- Carbohydrates: 6g
- Fiber: 2g

AVOCADO TOAST WITH POACHED EGG

Ingredients

- 1 slice of whole grain bread
- 1/2 ripe avocado
- 1 egg
- Salt and pepper to taste
- Optional toppings: red pepper flakes, chopped chives.

Instructions

- Fill a small saucepan with water and bring it to a simmer.
- Crack the egg into a small bowl or cup.
- Create a gentle whirlpool in the water and carefully slide the egg into the center.
- Cook for about 3-4 minutes for a soft yolk, or longer for a firmer yolk.
- Remove the egg with a slotted spoon and place it on a paper towel to drain.
- While the egg is poaching, cut the avocado in half and remove the pit.
- Scoop out the flesh into a bowl and mash it with a fork.
- Toast the bread until golden brown and crispy.
- Spread the mashed avocado evenly onto the toasted bread.
- Place the poached egg on top.
- Season with additional salt and pepper if desired.
- Add any optional toppings like red pepper flakes, chopped chives, or a squeeze of lemon juice.
- Serve the avocado toast immediately and enjoy!

 Preparation Time : 5 min

 Total Time : 10 min

Servings : 1

Nutritional Info

- Calories: 300 kcal
- Protein: 10g
- Fat: 20g
- Carbohydrates: 25g
- Fiber: 10g

EGG MUFFINS WITH VEGGIES

Ingredients

- 6 eggs
- 1/4 cup diced bell peppers (any color)
- 1/4 cup diced onion
- 1/4 cup diced tomatoes
- 1/4 cup chopped spinach
- Salt and pepper to taste
- Cooking spray or olive oil for greasing

Instructions

- Preheat your oven to 350°F (175°C). Grease a muffin tin with cooking spray or olive oil.
- In a mixing bowl, crack the eggs and whisk them together until well beaten.
- Add the diced bell peppers, onions, tomatoes, and chopped spinach to the bowl. Season with salt and pepper, and stir until everything is evenly combined.
- Pour the egg mixture evenly into the prepared muffin tin, filling each cup about 3/4 full.
- Bake in the preheated oven for 15-20 minutes, or until the egg muffins are set and slightly golden on top.
- Once cooked, remove the muffin tin from the oven and allow the egg muffins to cool for a few minutes.
- Carefully remove the egg muffins from the muffin tin using a spoon or spatula.
- Serve warm, or allow them to cool completely before storing in an airtight container in the refrigerator for up to 3 days.

 Preparation Time : 10 min

 Total Time : 30 min

 Servings : 6

Nutritional Info

- Calories: 120 kcal
- Protein: 10g
- Carbohydrates: 4g
- Fat: 7g
- Fiber: 1g
- Sugar: 2g

BANANA OAT PANCAKES

Ingredients

- 1 ripe banana
- 1/2 cup rolled oats
- 2 eggs
- 1/2 teaspoon cinnamon
- 1/2 teaspoon vanilla extract
- Cooking spray or butter, for cooking
- Optional toppings: fresh berries, maple syrup, Greek yogurt

Instructions

- In a blender, combine the ripe banana, rolled oats, eggs, cinnamon, and vanilla extract. Blend until smooth.
- Heat a non-stick skillet or griddle over medium heat. Lightly coat with cooking spray or melt a small amount of butter.
- Pour the pancake batter onto the skillet, using about 1/4 cup for each pancake. Cook for 2-3 minutes, or until bubbles form on the surface.
- Flip the pancakes and cook for an additional 1-2 minutes, or until golden brown and cooked through.
- Remove the pancakes from the skillet and repeat with the remaining batter. Serve warm with your favorite toppings.

Preparation Time : 10 min

Total Time : 20 min

Servings : 2

Nutritional Info

- Calories: 250 kcal
- Protein: 10g
- Carbohydrates: 35g
- Fiber: 5g
- Sugars: 13g
- Fat: 8g

BERRY SMOOTHIE BOWL

Ingredients

- 1 ripe banana, frozen
- 1 cup mixed berries (such as strawberries, blueberries, raspberries)
- 1/2 cup unsweetened almond milk (or any milk of your choice)
- 1/4 cup rolled oats
- 1 tablespoon chia seeds
- Toppings of your choice (such as sliced bananas, fresh berries, granola, shredded coconut, nuts/seeds)

Instructions

- In a blender, combine the frozen banana, mixed berries, almond milk, rolled oats, and chia seeds.
- Blend until smooth and creamy, adding more almond milk if necessary to reach your desired consistency.
- Pour the smoothie into a bowl.
- Arrange your desired toppings on top of the smoothie.
- Serve immediately and enjoy!

 Preparation Time : 5 min

 Total Time : 0 min

 Servings : 1

Nutritional Info

- Calories: 250
- Protein: 5g
- Fat: 3g
- Carbohydrates: 50g
- Fiber: 10g

CHIA SEED BREAKFAST
PUDDING

Ingredients

- 2 tablespoons chia seeds
- 1/2 cup almond milk (or any milk of your choice)
- 1/2 teaspoon vanilla extract
- 1 tablespoon honey or maple syrup (optional)
- Fresh fruits (such as berries, sliced banana, or mango) for topping
- Nuts or seeds for topping (such as sliced almonds, chopped walnuts, or pumpkin seeds)

Instructions

- In a bowl or jar, combine chia seeds, almond milk, vanilla extract, and honey or maple syrup (if using). Stir well to combine.
- Cover the bowl or jar and refrigerate overnight, or for at least 4 hours, to allow the chia seeds to absorb the liquid and thicken into a pudding-like consistency.
- Once the chia seed pudding has thickened, give it a good stir.
- Serve the chia seed pudding chilled, topped with your favorite fruits, nuts, or seeds.
- Enjoy your nutritious and delicious Chia Seed Breakfast Pudding!

 Preparation Time : 5 min

 Total Time : 0 min

 Servings : 1

Nutritional Info

- Calories: 220 kcal
- Protein: 6g
- Carbohydrates: 20g
- Fat: 14g
- Fiber: 10g

GREEK YOGURT PARFAIT
WITH FRESH BERRIES

Ingredients

- 1 cup non-fat Greek yogurt
- 1/2 cup fresh strawberries, sliced
- 1/4 cup fresh blueberries
- 1/4 cup fresh raspberries
- 1 tablespoon honey (optional)
- 1/4 cup granola (optional for added texture)

Instructions

- Wash and slice the strawberries.
- Wash the blueberries and raspberries.
- In a glass or bowl, start by adding a layer of Greek yogurt at the bottom.
- Add a layer of sliced strawberries, blueberries, and raspberries on top of the yogurt.
- Drizzle a small amount of honey over the berries if using.
- Add another layer of Greek yogurt on top of the berries.
- Repeat the layers until all ingredients are used, finishing with berries on top.
- Sprinkle granola on top for added texture and crunch, if desired.
- Serve immediately or refrigerate for up to 1 hour to allow flavors to meld.

🥣 **Preparation Time : 10 min**

🕐 **Total Time : 10 min**

🍴 **Servings : 1**

Nutritional Info

Calories: 150
Protein: 15g
Carbohydrates: 20g
Fat: 2g
Fiber: 4g

EGG WHITE OMELET WITH SPINACH AND TOMATOES

Ingredients

- 4 large egg whites
- 1 cup fresh spinach, chopped
- 1/2 cup cherry tomatoes, halved
- 1/4 cup onions, finely chopped
- 1 clove garlic, minced
- 1 tablespoon olive oil
- Salt and pepper, to taste

Instructions

- Chop the spinach, halve the tomatoes, finely chop the onions, and mince the garlic.
- Heat olive oil in a skillet over medium heat.
- Add onions and garlic, cook for 2-3 minutes until soft.
- Add spinach and tomatoes, cook for 2-3 minutes until spinach is wilted. Remove from skillet.
- Whisk egg whites with a pinch of salt and pepper.
- Pour into the skillet and cook for 2 minutes until edges start to set.
- Spoon the spinach and tomato mix onto one half of the omelet.
- Fold the omelet in half over the vegetables.
- Cook for another 2-3 minutes until fully set.
- Slide onto a plate, garnish with herbs if desired, and serve immediately.

Preparation Time : 10 min

Total Time : 20 min

Servings : 1

Nutritional Info

- Calories: 110
- Protein: 12g
- Carbohydrates: 5g
- Fat: 4g
- Fiber: 2g

CHAPTER 2

LUNCHTIME FAVORITES

CUCUMBER AND TOMATO
SALAD WITH FETA

Ingredients

- 2 large cucumbers, sliced
- 2 cups cherry tomatoes, halved
- 1/2 cup crumbled feta cheese
- 2 tablespoons extra virgin olive oil
- 1 tablespoon red wine vinegar
- Salt and pepper to taste
- 2 tablespoons chopped fresh parsley (optional, for garnish)

Instructions

- In a large mixing bowl, combine the sliced cucumbers and halved cherry tomatoes.
- In a small bowl, whisk together the extra virgin olive oil and red wine vinegar to make the dressing. Season with salt and pepper to taste.
- Pour the dressing over the cucumber and tomato mixture. Toss gently to coat all the ingredients evenly.
- Sprinkle the crumbled feta cheese over the salad and gently toss again.
- Taste and adjust seasoning if needed.
- Transfer the salad to a serving dish and garnish with chopped fresh parsley, if desired.
- Serve immediately as a refreshing side dish or refrigerate until ready to serve.

Preparation Time : 10 min

Total Time : 10 min

Servings : 2

Nutritional Info

- Calories: 120
- Fat: 9g
- Carbohydrates: 7g
- Protein: 4g
- Fiber: 2g

SPINACH AND STRAWBERRY SALAD

Ingredients

- 6 cups fresh baby spinach leaves
- 1 pint strawberries, hulled and sliced
- 1/4 cup sliced almonds
- 1/4 cup crumbled feta cheese
- Balsamic vinaigrette dressing

Instructions

- Wash the spinach leaves thoroughly and pat them dry with paper towels or a clean kitchen towel.
- In a large salad bowl, combine the spinach leaves, sliced strawberries, sliced almonds, and crumbled feta cheese.
- Drizzle the desired amount of balsamic vinaigrette dressing over the salad. Toss gently to coat all the ingredients evenly.
- Serve immediately as a refreshing side salad or light meal.

Preparation Time : 10 min

Total Time : 10 min

Servings : 4

Nutritional Info

- Calories: 120
- Total Fat: 7g
- Saturated Fat: 1.5g
- Cholesterol: 5mg
- Sodium: 140mg
- Dietary Fiber: 4g

VEGGIE AND HUMMUS WRAP

Ingredients

- 1 whole wheat tortilla
- 1/4 cup hummus
- 1/2 cup mixed greens (such as spinach, arugula, or lettuce)
- 1/4 cup shredded carrots
- 1/4 cup sliced cucumber
- 1/4 cup bell pepper strips (any color)
- 1/4 cup cherry tomatoes, halved
- 1/4 avocado, sliced
- 1 tbsp red onion, thinly sliced
- Salt and pepper to taste

Instructions

- Wash and dry the mixed greens.
- Shred the carrots if not pre-shredded.
- Slice the cucumber, bell pepper, and avocado.
- Halve the cherry tomatoes.
- Thinly slice the red onion.
- Lay the whole wheat tortilla flat on a clean surface.
- Spread the hummus evenly over the tortilla, leaving a small border around the edges.
- Layer the mixed greens over the hummus.
- Add the shredded carrots, sliced cucumber, bell pepper strips, cherry tomatoes, avocado slices, and red onion on top of the greens.
- Drizzle with olive oil if using, and season with salt and pepper to taste.
- Fold the sides of the tortilla inward, then roll it up tightly from the bottom to the top, enclosing all the fillings.
- Cut the wrap in half, if desired, for easier handling.
- Serve immediately and enjoy!

 Preparation Time : 10 min

 Total Time : 10 min

 Servings : 1

Nutritional Info

- Calories: 250
- Protein: 7g
- Fat: 12g
- Carbohydrates: 29g
- Fiber: 8g

TURKEY LETTUCE WRAPS

Ingredients

- 1 lb ground turkey
- 1 small onion, finely chopped
- 1 bell pepper, finely chopped
- 2 tablespoons low-sodium soy sauce
- 1 teaspoon sesame oil
- 1 head of lettuce, leaves separated

Instructions

- Chop the onion and bell pepper.
- Separate and rinse the lettuce leaves.
- In a large skillet, cook the chopped onion over medium heat until translucent, about 2-3 minutes.
- Add the ground turkey and cook until browned, breaking it up with a spoon, about 5-7 minutes.
- Add the bell pepper to the skillet and cook for another 2 minutes.
- Stir in the soy sauce and sesame oil, cooking for an additional 2 minutes.
- Spoon the turkey mixture into the center of each lettuce leaf.
- Arrange the wraps on a platter and serve immediately.

Preparation Time : 10 min

Total Time : 20 min

Servings : 4

Nutritional Info

- Calories: 150
- Protein: 22g
- Carbohydrates: 5g
- Fat: 5g
- Fiber: 2g

GRILLED PORTOBELLO
MUSHROOM BURGER

Ingredients

- 4 large portobello mushroom caps
- 2 tablespoons balsamic vinegar
- 2 tablespoons olive oil
- 2 cloves garlic, minced
- Salt and pepper to taste
- 4 whole grain burger buns
- Toppings of your choice (lettuce, tomato, onion, avocado, etc.)

Instructions

- Preheat your grill to medium-high heat.
- Clean the portobello mushroom caps by gently wiping them with a damp cloth or paper towel to remove any dirt. Remove the stems if desired.
- In a small bowl, whisk together the balsamic vinegar, olive oil, minced garlic, salt, and pepper.
- Brush both sides of the mushroom caps generously with the balsamic vinegar mixture.
- Place the mushroom caps on the preheated grill, gill side down. Grill for about 4-5 minutes on each side, or until the mushrooms are tender and slightly charred.
- While the mushrooms are grilling, toast the burger buns on the grill until lightly golden brown.
- Assemble the burgers by placing each grilled portobello mushroom cap on a toasted bun. Add your favorite toppings such as lettuce, tomato, onion, avocado, or condiments.
- Serve immediately and enjoy your delicious Grilled Portobello Mushroom Burgers!

Preparation Time : 10 min

Total Time : 20 min

Servings : 4

Nutritional Info

- Calories: 150 kcal
- Protein: 8g
- Fat: 6g
- Carbohydrates: 20g
- Fiber: 6g
- Sugar: 6g

ZUCCHINI NOODLES WITH PESTO

Ingredients

- 2 large zucchinis
- 1 cup fresh basil leaves
- 1/4 cup pine nuts
- 1/4 cup grated Parmesan cheese
- 2 cloves garlic, peeled
- 1/4 cup extra virgin olive oil
- Salt and pepper to taste

Instructions

- Use a spiralizer to create zucchini noodles (zoodles) from the zucchinis. If you don't have a spiralizer, you can use a vegetable peeler to make thin strips.
- In a food processor, combine the basil leaves, pine nuts, grated Parmesan cheese, and garlic. Pulse until finely chopped.
- With the food processor running, slowly add the olive oil until the mixture is smooth and creamy. Season with salt and pepper to taste.
- Heat a large skillet over medium-high heat. Add the zucchini noodles and cook for 2-3 minutes until they are tender but still slightly crisp. Do not overcook to avoid soggy noodles.
- Remove the skillet from the heat and add the pesto sauce to the zucchini noodles. Toss until the noodles are well coated with the pesto.
- Transfer the zoodles to serving plates and garnish with cherry tomatoes if desired.
- Serve immediately and enjoy your delicious and healthy Zucchini Noodles with Pesto!

 Preparation Time : 15 min

Total Time : 20 min

Servings : 2

Nutritional Info

- Calories: 210
- Protein: 5g
- Carbohydrates: 7g
- Fat: 18g
- Fiber: 2g

SPICY TUNA AND AVOCADO
BOWL

Ingredients

- 1 can (5 oz) of tuna in water, drained
- 1 ripe avocado, diced
- 1 cup cooked brown rice (optional, adjust points if included)
- 1 cup mixed greens
- 1/2 cup shredded carrots
- 1/2 cup sliced cucumber
- 1/4 cup chopped green onions
- 1 tbsp soy sauce (low sodium)
- 1 tsp sesame oil
- 1 tsp Sriracha (adjust to taste)
- 1 tbsp lime juice
- 1 tbsp sesame seeds

Instructions

- Prepare the Ingredients: Drain the tuna and place it in a medium bowl. Dice the avocado and set aside. Cook the brown rice if using.
- Make the Dressing: In a small bowl, whisk together the soy sauce, sesame oil, Sriracha, and lime juice.
- Combine Ingredients: In the bowl with the tuna, add the mixed greens, shredded carrots, sliced cucumber, chopped green onions, and diced avocado. Pour the dressing over the mixture.
- Mix Well: Gently toss all the ingredients together until evenly coated with the dressing.
- Serve: Divide the mixture into bowls, sprinkle with sesame seeds, and season with salt and pepper to taste. Serve immediately.
- Optional: Serve over a bed of cooked brown rice for a heartier meal.

 Preparation Time : 10 min

 Total Time : 10 min

Servings : 1

Nutritional Info

- Calories: 320 (without brown rice)
- Protein: 20g
- Carbohydrates: 14g
- Fat: 22g
- Fiber: 8g

CHICKEN CAESAR SALAD

Ingredients

- 2 boneless, skinless chicken breasts
- 1 tablespoon olive oil
- 1 teaspoon garlic powder
- Salt and pepper to taste
- 1 large head of romaine lettuce, chopped
- 1/2 cup cherry tomatoes, halved
- 1/4 cup grated Parmesan cheese
- 1/2 cup croutons (optional)
- Lemon wedges for garnish

Instructions

- Preheat your oven to 375°F (190°C).
- Rub the chicken breasts with olive oil, garlic powder, salt, and pepper.
- Place the chicken breasts on a baking sheet and bake for 20 minutes, or until the internal temperature reaches 165°F (74°C).
- Allow the chicken to rest for 5 minutes before slicing.
- While the chicken is baking, chop the romaine lettuce and place it in a large salad bowl.
- Add the halved cherry tomatoes and grated Parmesan cheese to the bowl.
- If using croutons, add them to the salad as well.
- Once the chicken has rested, slice it into thin strips.
- Arrange the sliced chicken on top of the salad.
- Serve the salad with lemon wedges on the side for squeezing over the top.
- Divide the salad into four servings.
- Enjoy your Chicken Caesar Salad without dressing, optionally squeezing fresh lemon juice over the top for extra flavor.

 Preparation Time : 15 min

 Total Time : 35 min

 Servings : 4

Nutritional Info

- Calories: 220
- Protein: 30g
- Carbohydrates: 8g
- Fat: 8g
- Fiber: 2g

QUINOA AND BLACK BEAN SALAD

Ingredients

- 1 cup quinoa, rinsed
- 1 can (15 oz) black beans, drained and rinsed
- 1 cup cherry tomatoes, halved
- 1 red bell pepper, diced
- 1/4 cup red onion, finely chopped
- 1/4 cup fresh cilantro, chopped
- Juice of 1 lime
- 2 tablespoons olive oil
- Salt and pepper to taste

Instructions

- Cook quinoa according to package instructions. Once cooked, fluff with a fork and let it cool to room temperature.
- In a large bowl, combine cooked quinoa, black beans, cherry tomatoes, red bell pepper, red onion, and cilantro.
- In a small bowl, whisk together lime juice, olive oil, salt, and pepper.
- Pour the dressing over the quinoa mixture and toss until well combined.
- Serve chilled or at room temperature. Optionally, top with avocado slices before serving.

Preparation Time : 15 min

Total Time : 30 min

Servings : 4

Nutritional Info

- Calories: 250
- Total Fat: 7g
- Saturated Fat: 1g
- Cholesterol: 0mg
- Sodium: 300mg

GRILLED CHICKEN AND VEGETABLE SALAD

Ingredients

- 2 boneless, skinless chicken breasts
- 2 tablespoons olive oil
- 1 teaspoon garlic powder
- Salt and pepper to taste
- 4 cups mixed salad greens
- 1 bell pepper, sliced
- 1 cup cherry tomatoes, halved
- 1 small red onion, thinly sliced
- 1/4 cup balsamic vinaigrette dressing

Instructions

- Preheat your grill to medium-high heat.
- In a small bowl, mix together olive oil, garlic powder, salt, and pepper. Brush this mixture onto both sides of the chicken breasts.
- Grill the chicken breasts for about 6-8 minutes per side, or until cooked through and no longer pink in the center. Remove from the grill and let them rest for a few minutes before slicing.
- While the chicken is cooking, prepare the vegetables. In a large bowl, toss together the mixed salad greens, bell pepper slices, cherry tomatoes, and red onion slices.
- Once the chicken has rested, slice it thinly.
- Arrange the grilled chicken slices on top of the salad vegetables.
- Drizzle the balsamic vinaigrette dressing over the salad.
- Serve immediately and enjoy!

 Preparation Time : 15 min

 Total Time : 30 min

 Servings : 4

Nutritional Info

- Calories: 250 kcal
- Protein: 25g
- Carbohydrates: 15g
- Fat: 10g
- Fiber: 5g

Chapter 3
Soups and Stews

BEEF AND VEGETABLE STEW

Ingredients

- 1 lb (450g) lean beef stew meat, cut into cubes
- 2 tablespoons olive oil
- 1 onion, diced
- 2 cloves garlic, minced
- 2 carrots, sliced
- 2 celery stalks, chopped
- 2 potatoes, diced
- 1 cup (240ml) beef broth
- 1 can (14 oz/400g) diced tomatoes
- 1 teaspoon dried thyme
- Salt and pepper to taste

Instructions

- Heat olive oil in a large pot over medium heat. Add the diced beef and cook until browned on all sides, about 5-7 minutes.
- Add the diced onion and minced garlic to the pot. Cook until the onions are translucent, about 3-4 minutes.
- Add the sliced carrots, chopped celery, and diced potatoes to the pot. Stir to combine.
- Pour in the beef broth and diced tomatoes with their juices. Add the dried thyme, salt, and pepper.
- Bring the stew to a boil, then reduce the heat to low. Cover and simmer for about 1.5 to 2 hours, or until the beef is tender and the vegetables are cooked through.
- Taste and adjust seasoning if needed.
- Serve hot, garnished with fresh herbs if desired.

 Preparation Time : 15 min

 Total Time : 2hrs 15 min

 Servings : 6

Nutritional Info

- Calories: 250 kcal
- Protein: 25g
- Carbohydrates: 20g
- Fat: 8g
- Fiber: 5g

SPICY BLACK BEAN SOUP

Ingredients

- 2 cans (15 oz each) black beans, drained and rinsed
- 1 tablespoon olive oil
- 1 onion, diced
- 2 cloves garlic, minced
- 1 red bell pepper, diced
- 1 jalapeño pepper, seeded and minced
- 1 teaspoon ground cumin
- 1 teaspoon chili powder
- 1/2 teaspoon smoked paprika
- 1/4 teaspoon cayenne pepper (adjust to taste)
- 4 cups vegetable broth
- 1 can (14.5 oz) diced tomatoes
- Salt and pepper to taste
- Juice of 1 lime

Instructions

- In a large pot, heat olive oil over medium heat. Add diced onion and cook until translucent, about 3-4 minutes.
- Add minced garlic, diced red bell pepper, and minced jalapeño pepper to the pot. Cook for another 2-3 minutes until fragrant.
- Stir in ground cumin, chili powder, smoked paprika, and cayenne pepper. Cook for 1 minute, stirring constantly.
- Add black beans, vegetable broth, and diced tomatoes to the pot. Bring to a simmer and let it cook for 20-25 minutes, stirring occasionally.
- Once the soup has simmered and flavors have melded, use an immersion blender to partially blend the soup until desired consistency is reached. Alternatively, you can transfer half of the soup to a blender and blend until smooth, then return it to the pot.
- Season with salt, pepper, and lime juice to taste. Adjust spices if necessary.
- Serve hot, garnished with fresh cilantro, a dollop of sour cream or Greek yogurt, avocado slices, and tortilla chips if desired.

 Preparation Time : 15 min

 Total Time : 45 min

Servings : 4

Nutritional Info

- Calories: 220 kcal
- Protein: 10g
- Fat: 2g
- Carbohydrates: 40g
- Fiber: 10g

SEAFOOD CHOWDER

Ingredients

- 1 lb (450g) shrimp, peeled and deveined
- 1 lb (450g) cod or white fish fillets, cut into bite-sized pieces
- 1 onion, finely chopped
- 2 cloves garlic, minced
- 2 celery stalks, diced
- 2 carrots, diced
- 2 potatoes, peeled and diced
- 4 cups (950ml) low-sodium fish or vegetable broth
- 1 cup (240ml) skim milk
- Salt and pepper to taste

Instructions

- Sauté Vegetables: In a large pot, sauté the onion, garlic, celery, and carrots over medium heat until softened, about 5 minutes.
- Add Broth and Potatoes: Add the broth and diced potatoes to the pot. Bring to a boil, then reduce the heat and simmer for 15 minutes, or until the potatoes are tender.
- Add Seafood: Stir in the shrimp and fish. Cook for another 5 minutes, or until the seafood is cooked through.
- Add Milk: Gradually stir in the skim milk. Simmer for an additional 5 minutes.
- Season and Serve: Season the chowder with salt and pepper to taste. Ladle the chowder into bowls, garnish with chopped fresh parsley, and serve hot.

 Preparation Time : 20 min

 Total Time : 50 min

 Servings : 6

Nutritional Info

- Calories: 200
- Protein: 25g
- Carbohydrates: 20g
- Fat: 4g
- Fiber: 3g

BUTTERNUT SQUASH SOUP

Ingredients

- 1 medium butternut squash, peeled, seeded, and diced
- 1 onion, chopped
- 2 cloves garlic, minced
- 2 carrots, peeled and chopped
- 4 cups vegetable broth
- 1 teaspoon ground cinnamon
- 1/2 teaspoon ground nutmeg
- Salt and pepper, to taste
- 2 tablespoons olive oil

Instructions

- In a large pot, heat olive oil over medium heat. Add chopped onions and cook until translucent, about 5 minutes.
- Add minced garlic and chopped carrots to the pot. Cook for another 3-4 minutes, until fragrant.
- Add diced butternut squash to the pot along with vegetable broth, ground cinnamon, and ground nutmeg. Season with salt and pepper to taste.
- Bring the mixture to a boil, then reduce heat to low. Cover and simmer for about 30-35 minutes, or until the butternut squash is tender.
- Once the squash is tender, remove the pot from heat. Use an immersion blender to puree the soup until smooth. Alternatively, you can carefully transfer the soup in batches to a blender and blend until smooth, then return it to the pot.
- Taste the soup and adjust seasoning if necessary.
- Serve the soup hot, garnished with fresh herbs if desired.

 Preparation Time : 15 min

 Total Time : 60 min

 Servings : 4

Nutritional Info

- Calories: 180 kcal
- Fat: 7g
- Carbohydrates: 30g
- Fiber: 6g
- Protein: 3g

TOMATO BASIL SOUP

Ingredients

- 2 tablespoons olive oil
- 1 medium onion, chopped
- 3 cloves garlic, minced
- 1 carrot, chopped
- 1 celery stalk, chopped
- 4 cups fresh tomatoes, chopped (or 2 cans diced tomatoes)
- 2 cups vegetable broth
- 1/2 cup fresh basil leaves, chopped
- Salt and pepper to taste

Instructions

- Heat 2 tablespoons of olive oil in a large pot over medium heat.
- Add 1 chopped onion, 1 chopped carrot, and 1 chopped celery stalk. Cook for about 5 minutes until softened.
- Add 3 minced garlic cloves and cook for 1 more minute.
- Add 4 cups of chopped fresh tomatoes (or 2 cans of diced tomatoes) and 2 cups of vegetable broth to the pot.
- Stir well and bring to a boil.
- Reduce the heat and let the soup simmer for 20 minutes.
- Remove the pot from the heat.
- Use an immersion blender to blend the soup until smooth (or carefully blend in batches in a regular blender).
- Stir in 1/2 cup of chopped fresh basil leaves.
- Add salt and pepper to taste.
- Simmer for an additional 5 minutes.
- Serve the soup hot and enjoy!

 Preparation Time : 10 min

 Total Time : 40 min

 Servings : 4

Nutritional Info

- Calories: 90
- Fat: 3g
- Carbohydrates: 15g
- Protein: 3g
- Fiber: 3g

MINESTRONE SOUP

Ingredients

- 1 tablespoon olive oil
- 1 onion, diced
- 2 carrots, diced
- 2 celery stalks, diced
- 2 cloves garlic, minced
- 1 can (14 oz) diced tomatoes
- 6 cups vegetable broth
- 1 can (15 oz) kidney beans, drained and rinsed
- 1 cup small pasta (such as ditalini or small shells)
- 2 cups chopped fresh spinach
- 1 teaspoon dried oregano
- 1 teaspoon dried basil
- Salt and pepper to taste

Instructions

- Heat olive oil in a large pot over medium heat. Add diced onion, carrots, and celery. Cook, stirring occasionally, for about 5 minutes or until vegetables are softened.
- Add minced garlic to the pot and cook for an additional 1-2 minutes, until fragrant.
- Pour in diced tomatoes and vegetable broth. Stir well to combine.
- Add drained kidney beans, pasta, dried oregano, and dried basil to the pot. Season with salt and pepper to taste. Bring the soup to a simmer.
- Simmer the soup uncovered for about 15-20 minutes, or until the pasta is cooked al dente and the vegetables are tender.
- Stir in chopped spinach and cook for an additional 2-3 minutes, until wilted.
- Taste and adjust seasoning if necessary. Serve hot, optionally topped with grated Parmesan cheese.

 Preparation Time : 15 min

 Total Time : 45 min

Servings : 6

Nutritional Info

- Calories: 180
- Total Fat: 2g
- Saturated Fat: 0.5g
- Cholesterol: 0mg
- Sodium: 600mg

CHICKEN AND VEGETABLE SOUP

Ingredients

- 1 tablespoon olive oil
- 1 onion, chopped
- 2 cloves garlic, minced
- 2 carrots, diced
- 2 celery stalks, diced
- 1 bell pepper, diced
- 1 teaspoon dried thyme
- 1 teaspoon dried oregano
- 4 cups low-sodium chicken broth
- 1 cup diced cooked chicken breast
- Salt and pepper to taste

Instructions

- Heat olive oil in a large pot over medium heat. Add chopped onion and minced garlic. Cook until softened, about 2-3 minutes.
- Add diced carrots, celery, and bell pepper to the pot. Cook for another 5 minutes, stirring occasionally, until vegetables are slightly tender.
- Stir in dried thyme and oregano. Cook for another minute to allow the herbs to become fragrant.
- Pour in the chicken broth and bring the mixture to a simmer. Let it cook for about 10 minutes, allowing the flavors to meld together.
- Add the diced cooked chicken breast to the pot. Simmer for an additional 5-10 minutes until the chicken is heated through and the vegetables are tender.
- Season the soup with salt and pepper to taste.
- Serve the chicken and vegetable soup hot, garnished with fresh chopped parsley if desired.

 Preparation Time : 15 min

 Total Time : 45 min

 Servings : 4

Nutritional Info

- Calories: 180 kcal
- Protein: 20g
- Carbohydrates: 15g
- Fat: 4g
- Fiber: 4g

CREAMY CARROT AND GINGER SOUP

Ingredients

- 1 lb (450g) carrots, peeled and chopped
- 1 onion, diced
- 2 cloves garlic, minced
- 1-inch piece of fresh ginger, peeled and grated
- 4 cups (1 liter) vegetable broth
- 1 cup (240ml) coconut milk
- Salt and pepper to taste

Instructions

- In a large pot, heat some olive oil over medium heat. Add the diced onion and minced garlic. Sauté until the onion is soft and translucent, about 3-4 minutes.
- Add the chopped carrots and grated ginger to the pot. Cook for another 2-3 minutes, stirring occasionally.
- Pour in the vegetable broth, ensuring the carrots are fully submerged. Bring the mixture to a boil, then reduce the heat to low. Cover and simmer for 15-20 minutes, or until the carrots are tender.
- Once the carrots are cooked, remove the pot from the heat. Use an immersion blender to puree the soup until smooth. Alternatively, transfer the soup in batches to a blender and blend until smooth.
- Return the pureed soup to the pot (if using a blender). Stir in the coconut milk until well combined. Season with salt and pepper to taste.
- Place the pot back on the stove over low heat, and gently warm the soup for another 5 minutes, stirring occasionally.
- Serve the creamy carrot and ginger soup hot, garnished with fresh cilantro or parsley if desired. Enjoy!

 Preparation Time : 10 min

 Total Time : 35 min

Servings : 4

Nutritional Info

- Calories: 150
- Protein: 2g
- Fat: 8g
- Carbohydrates: 18g
- Fiber: 4g

CABBAGE SOUP

Ingredients

- 1 tablespoon olive oil
- 1 onion, diced
- 3 cloves garlic, minced
- 1 small head cabbage, chopped
- 2 carrots, diced
- 2 stalks celery, sliced
- 1 can (14.5 ounces) diced tomatoes
- 6 cups vegetable broth
- 1 teaspoon dried thyme
- Salt and pepper to taste

Instructions

- Heat olive oil in a large pot over medium heat. Add diced onion and minced garlic. Sauté until onion is translucent, about 3-4 minutes.
- Add chopped cabbage, diced carrots, and sliced celery to the pot. Cook for 5 minutes, stirring occasionally, until vegetables begin to soften.
- Pour in diced tomatoes (including juices) and vegetable broth. Stir well to combine.
- Season the soup with dried thyme, salt, and pepper to taste. Bring to a boil, then reduce heat to low. Cover and simmer for 20 minutes, or until vegetables are tender.
- Taste and adjust seasoning if needed. Serve hot, garnished with chopped fresh parsley.

 Preparation Time : 15 min

 Total Time : 45 min

Servings : 6

Nutritional Info

- Calories: 120
- Total Fat: 1g
- Carbohydrates: 25g
- Protein: 5g
- Fiber: 7g
- Sodium: 650mg

LENTIL AND SPINACH STEW

Ingredients

- 1 cup dried green lentils, rinsed and drained
- 4 cups vegetable broth
- 1 onion, diced
- 2 cloves garlic, minced
- 1 teaspoon ground cumin
- 1 teaspoon ground coriander
- 1 teaspoon paprika
- 1/2 teaspoon turmeric
- 1/4 teaspoon cayenne pepper (optional)
- 2 cups chopped fresh spinach
- Salt and pepper to taste

Instructions

- In a large pot, combine the dried lentils and vegetable broth. Bring to a boil over medium-high heat.
- Reduce the heat to low and simmer for about 15 minutes, or until the lentils are just tender.
- In a separate pan, heat a little oil over medium heat. Add the diced onion and cook until softened, about 5 minutes.
- Add the minced garlic, ground cumin, ground coriander, paprika, turmeric, and cayenne pepper (if using) to the pan. Cook for another 2 minutes, stirring constantly, until fragrant.
- Transfer the onion and spice mixture to the pot with the lentils and broth. Stir to combine.
- Continue to simmer the stew for an additional 10 minutes, allowing the flavors to meld together.
- Stir in the chopped spinach and cook for another 2-3 minutes, until the spinach is wilted.
- Season the stew with salt and pepper to taste.
- Serve hot, garnished with fresh cilantro if desired and lemon wedges on the side for squeezing over the stew.

 Preparation Time : 15 min

 Total Time : 45 min

 Servings : 4

Nutritional Info

- Calories: 250
- Total Fat: 2g
- Saturated Fat: 0.5g
- Cholesterol: 0mg
- Sodium: 480mg
- Total Carbohydrate: 45g

Chapter 4

Savory Snacks and Sides

EDAMAME WITH SEA SALT

Ingredients

- 2 cups frozen edamame in pods
- 1 tablespoon sea salt (or to taste)
- Water for boiling

Instructions

- Fill a large pot with water and bring it to a boil over high heat.
- Once the water is boiling, add the frozen edamame pods to the pot.
- Boil for 5 minutes, or until the edamame pods are tender and easily open when squeezed.
- Drain the edamame in a colander and rinse under cold water to stop the cooking process.
- Transfer the edamame to a bowl and sprinkle with sea salt. Toss to evenly coat the pods with the salt.
- Serve immediately as a snack or appetizer.
- To eat, simply squeeze the edamame beans out of the pods and discard the pods.

 Preparation Time : 5 min

 Total Time : 15 min

 Servings : 4

Nutritional Info

- Calories: 120
- Protein: 12g
- Carbohydrates: 10g
- Fat: 5g
- Fiber: 4g
- Sodium: 150mg

CAULIFLOWER RICE PILAF

Ingredients

- 1 large head of cauliflower, riced
- 1 small onion, finely chopped
- 2 cloves garlic, minced
- 1 carrot, diced
- 1 red bell pepper, diced
- 1/2 cup green peas
- 2 tablespoons olive oil
- 1/4 cup low-sodium vegetable broth
- 1 teaspoon ground turmeric
- 1 teaspoon ground cumin
- Salt and pepper to taste

Instructions

- Rice the Cauliflower: Cut cauliflower into florets and pulse in a food processor until it looks like rice.
- Cook the Veggies: Heat olive oil in a large skillet over medium heat. Add onion and garlic, and cook for 2 minutes. Add carrot and bell pepper, and cook for another 5 minutes.
- Add Cauliflower Rice: Stir in the riced cauliflower, vegetable broth, and peas. Add turmeric, cumin, salt, and pepper.
- Finish Cooking: Cover and cook for 5-7 minutes, until the cauliflower is tender.
- Garnish and Serve: Sprinkle with fresh parsley and serve warm.

Preparation Time : 10 min

Total Time : 25 min

Servings : 4

Nutritional Info

- Calories: 110
- Protein: 3g
- Carbohydrates: 12g
- Dietary Fiber: 4g
- Sugars: 5g
- Fat: 6g

CRUNCHY CELERY AND APPLE SALAD

Ingredients

- 4 stalks of celery, thinly sliced
- 2 large apples (Granny Smith or Honeycrisp), cored and diced
- 1/4 cup walnuts, chopped (optional)
- 1/4 cup raisins (optional)
- 2 tablespoons lemon juice
- 1/2 teaspoon salt
- 1/4 teaspoon black pepper
- 1 tablespoon olive oil (optional)

Instructions

- Wash and thinly slice the celery stalks.
- Core and dice the apples into bite-sized pieces.
- In a large mixing bowl, combine the sliced celery and diced apples.
- If using, add the chopped walnuts and raisins to the bowl.
- Drizzle the lemon juice over the salad mixture to prevent the apples from browning.
- Season with salt and black pepper.
- Add the olive oil, if desired, for a richer flavor.
- Toss all ingredients together until well combined.
- Garnish with chopped parsley if desired.
- Serve the salad immediately to maintain its crunchiness.

🥣 **Preparation Time : 15 min**

🕐 **Total Time : 15 min**

🍴 **Servings : 4**

Nutritional Info

- Calories: 80
- Protein: 1g
- Carbohydrates: 18g
- Fat: 1g
- Fiber: 4g

GARLIC AND PARMESAN ROASTED BROCCOLI

Ingredients

- 1 large head of broccoli, cut into florets
- 3 cloves of garlic, minced
- 2 tablespoons olive oil
- 1/4 cup grated Parmesan cheese
- Salt and pepper to taste

Instructions

- Preheat oven to 400°F (200°C).
- Prepare the Broccoli:
- Cut broccoli into florets and place in a bowl.
- Add minced garlic, olive oil, salt, and pepper to the bowl. Toss to coat.
- Spread broccoli on a baking sheet and roast for 15-20 minutes, stirring halfway.
- Remove from oven and sprinkle with Parmesan cheese. Toss to coat.
- Serve hot.

 Preparation Time : 10 min

 Total Time : 30 min

Servings : 4

Nutritional Info

- Calories: 110
- Protein: 4g
- Carbohydrates: 8g
- Fat: 7g
- Fiber: 3g
- Sodium: 120mg

STUFFED BELL PEPPERS

Ingredients

- 4 large bell peppers, tops cut off and seeds removed
- 1 lb ground turkey or extra-lean ground beef
- 1 cup cooked quinoa or brown rice
- 1 medium onion, chopped
- 1 can (15 oz) diced tomatoes, drained
- 1 cup spinach, chopped
- 2 cloves garlic, minced
- 1 tsp dried oregano
- 1 tsp dried basil
- Salt and pepper to taste

Instructions

- Preheat Oven: Preheat oven to 375°F (190°C).
- Prepare Peppers: Cut tops off bell peppers and remove seeds. Set aside.
- Cook Filling: In a large pan, cook ground turkey until browned. Add onion and garlic; cook until onion is soft.
- Mix Ingredients: Add tomatoes, quinoa, spinach, oregano, basil, salt, and pepper to the pan. Stir and cook for 5 minutes.
- Stuff Peppers: Fill each bell pepper with the mixture.
- Bake Peppers: Place stuffed peppers in a baking dish, cover with foil, and bake for 25 minutes.
- Serve: Remove from oven and let cool slightly before serving.

 Preparation Time : 15 min

 Total Time : 45 min

 Servings : 4

Nutritional Info

- Calories: 150
- Protein: 20g
- Carbohydrates: 12g
- Fat: 3g
- Fiber: 4g

GUACAMOLE WITH VEGGIE STICKS

Ingredients

- 2 ripe avocados
- 1 small tomato, diced
- 1/4 cup red onion, finely chopped
- 1 jalapeño pepper, seeded and minced (optional for spice)
- 2 tablespoons fresh cilantro, chopped
- 1 tablespoon lime juice
- Salt and pepper to taste

Instructions

- Cut the avocados in half, remove the pits, and scoop the flesh into a mixing bowl.
- Mash the avocados with a fork until smooth or until your desired consistency is reached.
- Add the diced tomato, chopped red onion, minced jalapeño pepper (if using), chopped cilantro, and lime juice to the bowl with the mashed avocado.
- Season with salt and pepper to taste.
- Stir all the ingredients until well combined.
- Taste and adjust seasoning if necessary.
- Transfer the guacamole to a serving bowl and garnish with additional cilantro if desired.
- Serve the guacamole with assorted vegetable sticks for dipping.

 Preparation Time : 10 min

 Total Time : 10 min

Servings : 4

Nutritional Info

- Calories: 120
- Total Fat: 10g
- Saturated Fat: 1.5g
- Sodium: 250mg
- Total Carbohydrates: 8g
- Dietary Fiber: 6g

SPICED SWEET POTATO FRIES

Ingredients

- 2 large sweet potatoes
- 1 teaspoon paprika
- 1/2 teaspoon garlic powder
- 1/2 teaspoon onion powder
- 1/2 teaspoon ground cumin
- 1/4 teaspoon cayenne pepper (optional)
- Salt and pepper to taste

Instructions

- Preheat Oven: Preheat oven to 425°F (220°C). Line a baking sheet with parchment paper or spray with cooking spray.
- Cut Sweet Potatoes: Peel and cut sweet potatoes into thin fries.
- Season: Mix paprika, garlic powder, onion powder, cumin, cayenne pepper (if using), salt, and pepper in a large bowl. Add sweet potatoes and toss to coat.
- Bake: Spread fries on the baking sheet in a single layer. Bake for 20-25 minutes, turning halfway through, until golden and crispy.
- Serve: Let cool slightly and enjoy!

Preparation Time : 10 min

Total Time : 35 min

Servings : 4

Nutritional Info

- Calories: 120
- Protein: 2g
- Carbohydrates: 27g
- Fiber: 4g
- Fat: 0.5g

ROASTED CHICKPEAS

Ingredients

- 1 can (15 oz) chickpeas, drained and rinsed
- 1 tablespoon olive oil
- 1 teaspoon paprika
- 1 teaspoon garlic powder
- 1/2 teaspoon salt
- 1/4 teaspoon black pepper

Instructions

- Preheat Oven: Preheat your oven to 400°F (200°C).
- Dry Chickpeas: Pat the chickpeas dry with paper towels.
- Season Chickpeas: In a bowl, mix chickpeas with olive oil, paprika, garlic powder, salt, and pepper.
- Bake: Spread chickpeas on a baking sheet. Bake for 35-40 minutes, shaking the pan halfway through.
- Cool: Let cool for a few minutes before serving.

 Preparation Time : 10 min

 Total Time : 50 min

 Servings : 4

Nutritional Info

- Calories: 120
- Protein: 6g
- Fat: 2g
- Carbohydrates: 20g
- Fiber: 6g

BAKED KALE CHIPS

Ingredients

- 1 bunch of kale
- 1 tablespoon olive oil (optional)
- 1 teaspoon sea salt

Instructions

- Preheat oven to 300°F (150°C).
- Prepare kale: Wash and dry kale. Tear into bite-sized pieces, removing stems.
- Season: Toss kale with olive oil (if using) and salt.
- Bake: Spread kale on a baking sheet in a single layer. Bake for 20 minutes, until edges are brown.
- Cool and serve: Let cool for a few minutes to crisp up. Enjoy!

 Preparation Time : 10 min

 Total Time : 30 min

Servings : 4

Nutritional Info

- Calories: 50
- Total Fat: 2g (with olive oil)
- Saturated Fat: 0g
- Cholesterol: 0mg
- Sodium: 200mg
- Total Carbohydrates: 8g

MARINATED MUSHROOM
SKEWERS

Ingredients

- 1 lb (450g) button mushrooms, cleaned and stems trimmed
- 2 tbsp olive oil
- 3 tbsp balsamic vinegar
- 2 cloves garlic, minced
- 1 tsp dried thyme
- 1 tsp dried rosemary
- Salt and pepper to taste

Instructions

- Mix olive oil, balsamic vinegar, garlic, thyme, rosemary, salt, and pepper in a bowl.
- Add mushrooms and toss to coat. Let sit for 10 minutes.
- If using wooden skewers, soak them in water for 10 minutes.
- Thread mushrooms onto skewers.
- Preheat grill to medium-high.
- Grill skewers for 5-7 minutes per side, until mushrooms are tender.
- Remove from grill and enjoy warm.

Preparation Time : 10 min

Total Time : 20 min

Servings : 4

Nutritional Info

- Calories: 80
- Protein: 2g
- Carbohydrates: 6g
- Fat: 5g
- Fiber: 2g
- Sugar: 3g

Chapter 5
Delicious Dinners

BEEF AND BROCCOLI STIR-FRY

Ingredients

- 1 lb (450g) lean beef steak, thinly sliced
- 2 cups broccoli florets
- 1 red bell pepper, thinly sliced
- 1 onion, thinly sliced
- 3 cloves garlic, minced
- 2 tbsp low-sodium soy sauce
- 1 tbsp oyster sauce
- 1 tbsp sesame oil
- 1 tbsp cornstarch
- 1 tsp fresh ginger, grated
- 2 tbsp vegetable oil
- Salt and pepper, to taste

Instructions

- In a bowl, mix soy sauce, oyster sauce, sesame oil, cornstarch, and grated ginger.
- Add beef to the marinade and let it sit for 10 minutes.
- Heat vegetable oil in a skillet or wok over medium-high heat.
- Add minced garlic and cook until fragrant, about 30 seconds.
- Add marinated beef and cook until browned, about 3 minutes. Remove beef.
- In the same skillet, add more oil if needed, then add broccoli, bell pepper, and onion. Cook for 3-4 minutes until tender-crisp.
- Return beef to the skillet, stir together, and cook for 2 minutes to heat through.
- Season with salt and pepper.
- Garnish with sesame seeds and green onions if desired.
- Serve hot over rice or noodles.

 Preparation Time : 15 min

 Total Time : 30 min

 Servings : 4

Nutritional Info

- Calories: 250
- Protein: 25g
- Carbohydrates: 12g
- Fat: 11g
- Fiber: 4g

TURKEY MEATBALLS WITH ZOODLES

Ingredients

- 1 lb ground turkey
- 1/4 cup grated Parmesan cheese
- 1 large egg
- 2 cloves garlic, minced
- 1/4 cup chopped parsley
- 1 tsp dried oregano
- 1/2 tsp salt
- 1/4 tsp black pepper
- 4 medium zucchinis, spiralized
- 2 tbsp olive oil
- 1 clove garlic, minced
- Salt and pepper to taste

Instructions

- Mix turkey, Parmesan, egg, minced garlic, parsley, oregano, salt, and pepper in a bowl.
- Shape into 1-inch meatballs.
- Heat a large skillet over medium-high heat with a bit of olive oil.
- Cook meatballs until browned and cooked through, about 10-12 minutes.
- Remove meatballs from the skillet.
- In the same skillet, heat 2 tbsp olive oil over medium heat.
- Add minced garlic and cook for 1 minute.
- Add spiralized zucchini and cook for 3-5 minutes until tender.
- Season with salt and pepper.
- Return meatballs to the skillet and add marinara sauce.
- Heat until warm.
- Serve meatballs and sauce over zoodles.

🥣	**Preparation Time : 20 min**
🕐	**Total Time : 45 min**
🍴	**Servings : 4**

Nutritional Info

- Calories: 250
- Protein: 30g
- Carbohydrates: 10g
- Fat: 10g
- Fiber: 3g

VEGGIE STIR-FRY WITH TOFU

Ingredients

- 1 block (14 oz) firm tofu, cubed
- 2 tablespoons soy sauce (low sodium)
- 1 tablespoon olive oil
- 2 bell peppers, sliced
- 1 cup broccoli florets
- 1 cup snap peas
- 2 cloves garlic, minced
- 1 tablespoon fresh ginger, grated
- 2 tablespoons vegetable broth (low sodium)
- Salt and pepper to taste

Instructions

- Drain, pat dry, and cube the tofu. Toss with 1 tablespoon soy sauce.
- Heat olive oil in a large pan over medium-high heat. Cook tofu until golden brown, about 5-7 minutes. Remove from pan.
- In the same pan, add garlic and ginger, sauté for 30 seconds.
- Add bell peppers, broccoli, and snap peas. Stir-fry for 4-5 minutes until tender-crisp.
- Return tofu to pan. Add 1 tablespoon soy sauce and vegetable broth. Stir and cook for 2-3 minutes.
- Season with salt and pepper. Serve warm.

 Preparation Time : 10 min

 Total Time : 20 min

 Servings : 4

Nutritional Info

- Calories: 180
- Protein: 12g
- Carbohydrates: 16g
- Fat: 8g
- Fiber: 5g

HERB-CRUSTED CHICKEN BREAST

Ingredients

- 4 boneless, skinless chicken breasts
- 2 tablespoons olive oil
- 1/4 cup fresh parsley, chopped
- 1/4 cup fresh basil, chopped
- 1/4 cup fresh thyme, chopped
- 2 cloves garlic, minced
- 1 teaspoon salt
- 1/2 teaspoon black pepper
- 1 teaspoon lemon zest

Instructions

- Preheat Oven: Preheat your oven to 400°F (200°C).
- Prepare Herb Mixture: In a small bowl, combine the chopped parsley, basil, thyme, minced garlic, salt, black pepper, and lemon zest.
- Prepare Chicken: Pat the chicken breasts dry with paper towels. Rub each breast with olive oil, ensuring they are evenly coated.
- Coat with Herbs: Press the herb mixture onto both sides of each chicken breast, making sure they are well coated.
- Bake Chicken: Place the chicken breasts on a baking sheet lined with parchment paper or in a lightly greased baking dish.
- Cook: Bake in the preheated oven for 25 minutes, or until the internal temperature of the chicken reaches 165°F (74°C) and the exterior is golden brown.
- Rest and Serve: Let the chicken rest for 5 minutes before serving to allow the juices to redistribute.

 Preparation Time : 15 min

 Total Time : 40 min

 Servings : 4

Nutritional Info

- Calories: 220
- Protein: 28g
- Carbohydrates: 2g
- Fat: 11g

SPAGHETTI SQUASH WITH MARINARA SAUCE

Ingredients

- 1 medium spaghetti squash
- 2 cups marinara sauce
- 2 tablespoons olive oil
- Salt and pepper to taste

Instructions

- Preheat oven to 400°F (200°C).
- Cut spaghetti squash in half lengthwise and remove seeds.
- Drizzle olive oil over cut sides of squash and season with salt and pepper.
- Place squash halves cut-side down on a baking sheet.
- Roast squash in oven for 35-40 minutes, until tender.
- While squash is roasting, heat marinara sauce in a saucepan on medium heat.
- Once squash is done, remove from oven and let cool slightly.
- Use a fork to scrape flesh into spaghetti-like strands onto a plate.
- Pour heated marinara sauce over spaghetti squash.
- Serve hot and enjoy!

 Preparation Time : 10 min

 Total Time : 50 min

 Servings : 4

Nutritional Info

- Calories: 150
- Total Fat: 6g
- Total Carbohydrates: 24g
- Protein: 3g

BALSAMIC GLAZED CHICKEN BREAST

Ingredients

- 4 boneless, skinless chicken breasts
- 1/2 cup balsamic vinegar
- 2 tablespoons honey
- 2 cloves garlic, minced
- 1 teaspoon dried thyme
- Salt and pepper
- 1 tablespoon olive oil

Instructions

- Mix balsamic vinegar, honey, minced garlic, and dried thyme in a bowl.
- Pour over chicken breasts and let sit for 10 minutes.
- Heat olive oil in a skillet over medium-high heat.
- Remove chicken from marinade (save marinade) and season with salt and pepper.
- Cook chicken for 5 minutes on each side until browned.
- Pour the reserved marinade into the skillet.
- Cook for another 10 minutes, turning chicken to coat with glaze, until chicken is cooked through (165°F internal temperature).
- Let chicken rest for 5 minutes.
- Drizzle with remaining glaze from the skillet.

 Preparation Time : 10 min

 Total Time : 30 min

 Servings : 4

Nutritional Info

- Calories: 200
- Protein: 30g
- Fat: 4g
- Carbohydrates: 8g

GRILLED VEGETABLE KEBABS

Ingredients

- 1 red bell pepper, cut into chunks
- 1 yellow bell pepper, cut into chunks
- 1 zucchini, sliced into rounds
- 1 red onion, cut into chunks
- 8 cherry tomatoes
- 8 button mushrooms
- 2 tablespoons olive oil
- 1 teaspoon dried oregano
- 1 teaspoon dried basil
- Salt and pepper to taste

Instructions

- Wash and cut the vegetables as indicated.
- If using wooden skewers, soak them in water for at least 10 minutes to prevent burning.
- In a large bowl, combine the olive oil, dried oregano, dried basil, salt, and pepper.
- Add the cut vegetables to the bowl and toss to coat them evenly with the marinade.
- Thread the marinated vegetables onto the skewers, alternating between different types of vegetables for a colorful presentation.
- Preheat your grill to medium-high heat.
- Place the kebabs on the preheated grill.
- Grill for about 10-15 minutes, turning occasionally, until the vegetables are tender and slightly charred.
- Remove the kebabs from the grill and serve immediately.

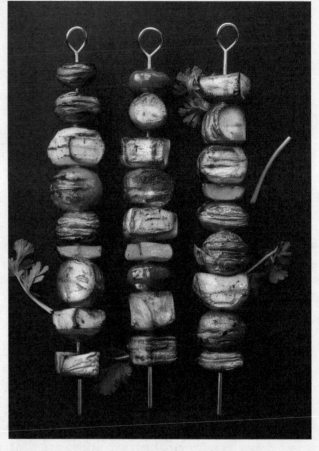

 Preparation Time : 20 min

 Total Time : 35min

 Servings : 4

Nutritional Info

- Calories: 90
- Protein: 3g
- Carbohydrates: 15g
- Fat: 3g
- Fiber: 5g

BAKED COD WITH LEMON AND DILL

Ingredients

- 4 cod fillets (about 6 ounces each)
- 2 tablespoons olive oil
- 2 cloves garlic, minced
- 1 tablespoon fresh dill, chopped
- 1 lemon, thinly sliced
- Salt and pepper to taste

Instructions

- Preheat your oven to 375°F (190°C).
- Place the cod fillets on a baking dish lined with parchment paper or lightly greased.
- In a small bowl, mix together the olive oil, minced garlic, and chopped dill.
- Drizzle the olive oil mixture over the cod fillets, making sure they are evenly coated.
- Season the cod fillets with salt and pepper to taste.
- Place lemon slices on top of each cod fillet.
- Bake in the preheated oven for about 15-20 minutes, or until the cod is cooked through and flakes easily with a fork.
- Remove from the oven and serve hot, garnished with additional fresh dill if desired.

 Preparation Time : 10 min

Total Time : 30 min

 Servings : 4

Nutritional Info

- Calories: 150 kcal
- Protein: 25g
- Carbohydrates: 2g
- Fat: 4g
- Fiber: 0.5g
- Sugar: 0g

BAKED LEMON HERB SALMON

Ingredients

- 4 salmon fillets (about 6 oz each)
- 2 tablespoons olive oil
- 2 lemons (one for juice, one for slices)
- 3 cloves garlic, minced
- 2 tablespoons fresh parsley, chopped
- 1 tablespoon fresh dill, chopped
- 1 teaspoon salt
- 1/2 teaspoon black pepper

Instructions

- Preheat your oven to 400°F (200°C).
- Place the salmon fillets on a baking sheet lined with parchment paper.
- In a small bowl, mix the olive oil, juice of one lemon, minced garlic, chopped parsley, chopped dill, salt, and black pepper.
- Brush the marinade generously over each salmon fillet. Let it sit for about 10 minutes to allow the flavors to infuse.
- Slice the second lemon into thin rounds and place a couple of slices on top of each salmon fillet.
- Bake in the preheated oven for 20 minutes, or until the salmon is cooked through and flakes easily with a fork.
- Remove from the oven and transfer to plates. Serve immediately, optionally garnished with extra fresh herbs and lemon wedges.

Preparation Time : 10 min

Total Time : 30 min

Servings : 4

Nutritional Info

- Calories: 230
- Protein: 25g
- Fat: 14g
- Carbohydrates: 2g
- Fiber: 1g

GRILLED SHRIMP SKEWERS

Ingredients

- 1 lb large shrimp, peeled and deveined
- 2 cloves garlic, minced
- 2 tbsp olive oil
- 1 tbsp lemon juice
- 1 tsp smoked paprika
- Salt and pepper to taste
- Fresh parsley, chopped (for garnish)

Instructions

- Marinate the Shrimp: In a large bowl, combine minced garlic, olive oil, lemon juice, smoked paprika, salt, and pepper. Add the shrimp and toss to coat. Let it marinate for 10 minutes.
- Prepare the Skewers: If using wooden skewers, soak them in water for 10 minutes to prevent burning. Thread the shrimp onto the skewers, leaving a little space between each shrimp.
- Preheat the Grill: Preheat the grill to medium-high heat.
- Grill the Shrimp: Place the shrimp skewers on the grill. Cook for 2-3 minutes per side, until the shrimp are opaque and cooked through.
- Serve: Remove the skewers from the grill and transfer to a serving platter. Garnish with chopped fresh parsley and lemon wedges. Serve immediately.

 Preparation Time : 15 min

 Total Time : 25 min

 Servings : 4

Nutritional Info

- Calories: 150
- Protein: 23g
- Carbohydrates: 2g
- Fat: 6g
- Fiber: 0g

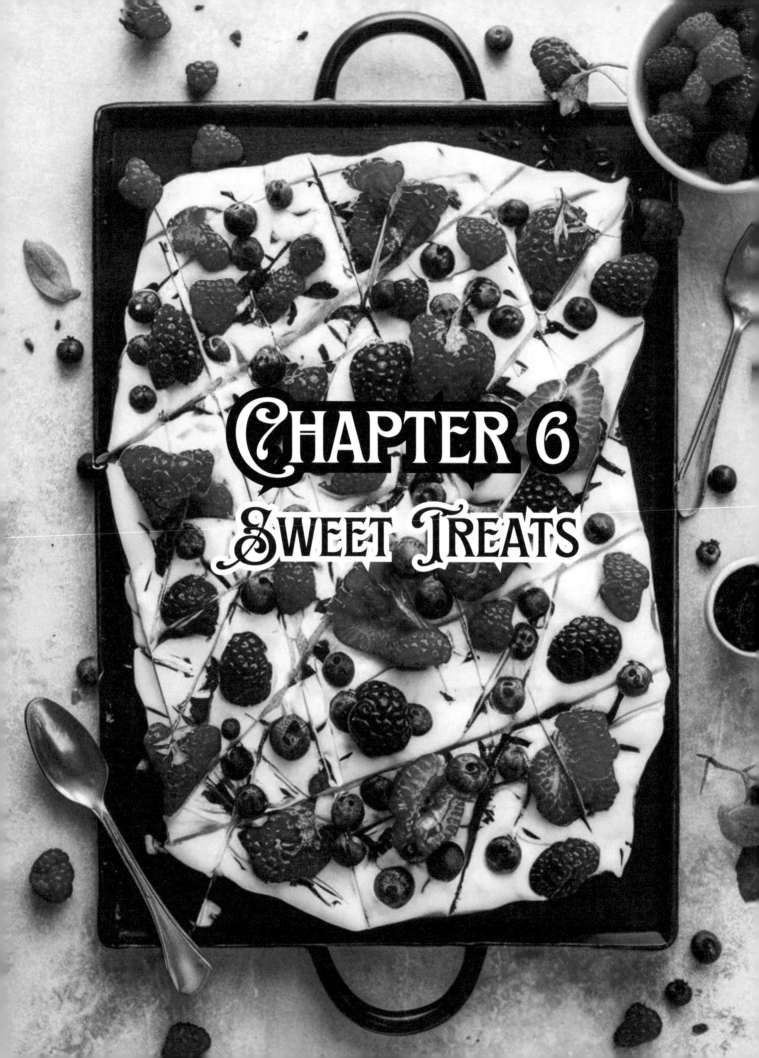

Chapter 6
Sweet Treats

MIXED BERRY SORBET

Ingredients

- 3 cups mixed berries (such as strawberries, blueberries, raspberries)
- 1/4 cup honey or maple syrup (optional)
- 2 tablespoons lemon juice

 Preparation Time : 10 min

 Total Time : 0 min

Servings : 4

Instructions

- Blend: Put the mixed berries, honey or maple syrup (if using), and lemon juice in a blender or food processor.
- Blend Again: Blend until smooth.
- Freeze: Pour the mixture into a shallow dish or pan. Cover and freeze for 3-4 hours, or until partially frozen.
- Scrape and Blend: Once partially frozen, scrape the mixture with a fork to break it up into icy flakes. Blend again until smooth.
- Freeze Again: Return the mixture to the dish or pan. Cover and freeze for another 2-3 hours, or until firm.
- Serve: Scoop the sorbet into bowls or glasses.
- Enjoy: Garnish with fresh mint leaves if desired, then serve and enjoy!

Nutritional Info

- Calories: Approximately 80 kcal
- Carbohydrates: Approximately 20 g
- Fiber: Approximately 3 g
- Sugars: Approximately 15 g
- Fat: Approximately 0 g

APPLE CINNAMON COMPOTE

Ingredients

- 4 medium apples, peeled, cored, and chopped
- 1 tablespoon lemon juice
- 1/4 cup water
- 2 tablespoons honey or maple syrup (optional)
- 1 teaspoon ground cinnamon
- 1/2 teaspoon vanilla extract (optional)

Instructions

- In a medium saucepan, combine the chopped apples, lemon juice, and water.
- Bring the mixture to a simmer over medium heat.
- Stir in the honey or maple syrup (if using), ground cinnamon, and vanilla extract (if using).
- Reduce the heat to low and let the mixture cook uncovered for about 15-20 minutes, or until the apples are soft and the liquid has thickened slightly, stirring occasionally.
- Once the apples are cooked to your desired consistency, remove the saucepan from the heat.
- Allow the compote to cool slightly before serving. You can serve it warm or chilled, depending on your preference.
- Enjoy the apple cinnamon compote on its own, or use it as a topping for yogurt, oatmeal, pancakes, or ice cream.

 Preparation Time : 10 min

 Total Time : 30 min

 Servings : 4

Nutritional Info

- Calories: 80 kcal
- Carbohydrates: 20 g
- Fiber: 4 g
- Sugars: 15 g
- Fat: 0 g
- Protein: 0 g

PEACH AND RASPBERRY CRUMBLE

Ingredients

- 1 ripe peach, sliced
- 1/2 cup fresh raspberries
- 1 tablespoon lemon juice
- 2 tablespoons granulated sugar (or sweetener of choice)
- 1/4 cup rolled oats
- 2 tablespoons all-purpose flour
- 1 tablespoon brown sugar
- 1/4 teaspoon ground cinnamon
- 2 tablespoons unsalted butter, chilled and cubed

Instructions

- Preheat your oven to 375°F (190°C). Lightly grease a small baking dish or individual ramekins.
- In a bowl, toss together the sliced peach, raspberries, lemon juice, and granulated sugar until well combined. Transfer the fruit mixture to the prepared baking dish or ramekins, spreading it out evenly.
- In another bowl, mix together the rolled oats, all-purpose flour, brown sugar, and ground cinnamon.
- Using your fingers, incorporate the chilled cubed butter into the oat mixture until it resembles coarse crumbs.
- Sprinkle the oat mixture evenly over the fruit in the baking dish or ramekins.
- Place the baking dish or ramekins in the preheated oven and bake for about 25-30 minutes, or until the fruit is bubbly and the crumble topping is golden brown.
- Remove from the oven and let it cool for a few minutes before serving.
- Serve warm as is or with a scoop of vanilla frozen yogurt or a dollop of whipped cream, if desired.

Preparation Time : 15 min

Total Time : 45 min

Servings : 1

Nutritional Info

- Calories: 250 kcal
- Carbohydrates: 40g
- Protein: 3g
- Fat: 10g
- Fiber: 5g

BAKED APPLES WITH CINNAMON

Ingredients

- 4 medium-sized apples
- 1 teaspoon ground cinnamon

Instructions

- Preheat your oven to 375°F (190°C).
- Wash the apples and remove the cores, leaving the bottoms intact to hold the filling.
- Place the cored apples in a baking dish.
- Sprinkle ground cinnamon evenly over each apple.
- Bake for 25 minutes, or until the apples are tender.
- Serve warm as is or with a dollop of Greek yogurt or a scoop of vanilla ice cream, if desired.

 **Preparation Time : 5 min**

 Total Time : 30 min

Servings : 4

Nutritional Info

- Calories: 120 kcal
- Total Fat: 0.5g
- Carbohydrates: 31g
- Fiber: 5g
- Sugars: 24g
- Protein: 0.5g

BLUEBERRY AND LEMON SORBET

Ingredients

- 2 cups fresh blueberries
- 1/2 cup water
- 1/2 cup granulated sugar
- Zest and juice of 1 lemon

Instructions

- Combine Ingredients: In a saucepan, mix blueberries, water, and sugar. Heat on medium until sugar dissolves and blueberries soften (about 5 minutes).
- Blend: Pour mixture into a blender, add lemon zest and juice, blend until smooth.
- Strain (Optional): If desired, strain mixture through a sieve for smoother texture.
- Chill and Freeze: Cool mixture in the fridge for 2 hours. Pour into a shallow dish, freeze for 4-6 hours. Stir every hour.
- Serve: Scoop into bowls, garnish with blueberries or lemon zest. Enjoy!

Preparation Time : 10 min

Total Time : 15 min

Servings : 4

Nutritional Info

- Calories: 80 kcal
- Fat: 0g
- Carbohydrates: 20g
- Fiber: 3g
- Sugars: 14g
- Protein: 1g

MANGO AND PINEAPPLE SALAD

Ingredients

- 1 ripe mango, peeled and diced
- 1 cup fresh pineapple chunks
- 1/4 cup red onion, finely chopped
- 1/4 cup fresh cilantro, chopped
- Juice of 1 lime
- Salt and pepper to taste

Instructions

- In a large mixing bowl, combine the diced mango, pineapple chunks, chopped red onion, and chopped cilantro.
- Squeeze the lime juice over the fruit mixture.
- Season with salt and pepper to taste.
- Gently toss the ingredients until everything is evenly coated with lime juice and seasoning.
- Serve immediately as a refreshing side dish or as a topping for grilled chicken or fish.

 Preparation Time : 10 min

 Total Time : 0 min

 Servings : 4

Nutritional Info

- Calories: 80 kcal
- Protein: 1g
- Carbohydrates: 21g
- Fat: 0g
- Fiber: 3g
- Sugar: 16g
- Sodium: 5mg

FROZEN YOGURT BARK WITH BERRIES

Ingredients

- 2 cups plain Greek yogurt
- 2 tablespoons honey or maple syrup
- 1 teaspoon vanilla extract
- 1 cup mixed berries (such as strawberries, blueberries, and raspberries)
- Optional: 2 tablespoons shredded coconut or chopped nuts for toppin

Instructions

- In a mixing bowl, combine the Greek yogurt, honey (or maple syrup), and vanilla extract. Stir until well combined.
- Line a baking sheet with parchment paper or a silicone baking mat.
- Pour the yogurt mixture onto the prepared baking sheet, spreading it evenly to about ¼ inch thickness.
- Scatter the mixed berries evenly over the yogurt mixture. Press them gently into the yogurt.
- If desired, sprinkle shredded coconut or chopped nuts over the top for added texture and flavor.
- Place the baking sheet in the freezer and let the yogurt bark freeze for at least 2 hours, or until completely firm.
- Once frozen, remove the baking sheet from the freezer and break the yogurt bark into pieces using your hands or a knife.
- Serve immediately as a refreshing snack or dessert. Store any leftovers in an airtight container in the freezer.

 Preparation Time : 10 min

 Total Time : 2hrs 10 min

Servings : 6

Nutritional Info

- Calories: 110 kcal
- Total Fat: 2g
- Saturated Fat: 1g
- Cholesterol: 5mg
- Sodium: 25mg
- Total Carbohydrates: 14g

CHOCOLATE DIPPED STRAWBERRIES

Ingredients

- 1 pint of fresh strawberries, washed and dried
- 4 oz (about 120g) of dark chocolate chips or chopped dark chocolate (70% cocoa or higher)

Instructions

- Line a baking sheet with parchment paper.
- In a microwave-safe bowl, melt the dark chocolate chips in 30-second intervals, stirring in between, until smooth and fully melted.
- Hold each strawberry by the stem and dip it into the melted chocolate, swirling to coat it partially.
- Place the dipped strawberries onto the prepared baking sheet.
- Repeat with the remaining strawberries.
- Place the baking sheet in the refrigerator for about 15-20 minutes or until the chocolate sets.
- Once the chocolate has hardened, transfer the chocolate-dipped strawberries to a serving plate.
- Serve immediately as a delicious and healthy dessert option.

 Preparation Time : 10 min

 Total Time : 15 min

 Servings : 4

Nutritional Info

- Calories: 120
- Total Fat: 7g
- Saturated Fat: 4g
- Cholesterol: 0mg
- Sodium: 5mg
- Total Carbohydrates: 15g

GRILLED PINEAPPLE WITH CINNAMON

Ingredients

- 1 ripe pineapple, peeled and cored
- 1 teaspoon ground cinnamon

Instructions

- Preheat your grill to medium-high heat.
- Slice the pineapple into rings or wedges, about 1/2 inch thick.
- Sprinkle both sides of the pineapple slices with ground cinnamon.
- Place the pineapple slices on the preheated grill.
- Grill for 3-4 minutes on each side, or until grill marks appear and the pineapple is heated through.
- Remove from the grill and serve hot.

 Preparation Time : 10 min

 Total Time : 5 min

 Servings : 2

Nutritional Info

- Calories: 90
- Total Fat: 0g
- Saturated Fat: 0g
- Cholesterol: 0mg
- Sodium: 0mg
- Total Carbohydrates: 23g

MIXED BERRY SORBET

Ingredients

- 3 cups mixed berries (such as strawberries, blueberries, raspberries)
- 1/4 cup honey or maple syrup (optional)
- 2 tablespoons lemon juice

Instructions

- Blend: Put the mixed berries, honey or maple syrup (if using), and lemon juice in a blender or food processor.
- Blend Again: Blend until smooth.
- Freeze: Pour the mixture into a shallow dish or pan. Cover and freeze for 3-4 hours, or until partially frozen.
- Scrape and Blend: Once partially frozen, scrape the mixture with a fork to break it up into icy flakes. Blend again until smooth.
- Freeze Again: Return the mixture to the dish or pan. Cover and freeze for another 2-3 hours, or until firm.
- Serve: Scoop the sorbet into bowls or glasses.
- Enjoy: Garnish with fresh mint leaves if desired, then serve and enjoy!

 Preparation Time : 10 min

 Total Time : 0 min

Servings : 4

Nutritional Info

- Calories: Approximately 80 kcal
- Carbohydrates: Approximately 20 g
- Fiber: Approximately 3 g
- Sugars: Approximately 15 g
- Fat: Approximately 0 g

Chapter 7
Drinks and Smoothies

WATERMELON COOLER

Ingredients

- 2 cups of diced seedless watermelon
- 1/2 cup of fresh lime juice
- 1 tablespoon of honey or agave syrup (optional)
- Ice cubes
- Fresh mint leaves for garnish (optional)

Instructions

- In a blender, combine the diced watermelon, lime juice, and honey (if using).
- Blend until smooth and well combined.
- Taste and adjust sweetness if necessary by adding more honey.
- Fill a glass with ice cubes.
- Pour the watermelon mixture over the ice cubes.
- Garnish with fresh mint leaves if desired.
- Serve immediately and enjoy!

Preparation Time : 5 min

Total Time : 10 min

Servings : 1

Nutritional Info

- Calories: 70 kcal
- Total Fat: 0 g
- Saturated Fat: 0 g
- Cholesterol: 0 mg
- Sodium: 2 mg
- Total Carbohydrates: 18 g

CUCUMBER MINT WATER

Ingredients

- 1 medium cucumber, thinly sliced
- 1/4 cup fresh mint leaves
- 1 lemon, thinly sliced
- 4 cups cold water
- Ice cubes (optional)

Instructions

- In a large pitcher, add the sliced cucumber, fresh mint leaves, and lemon slices.
- Pour cold water over the ingredients in the pitcher.
- Stir gently to combine.
- Refrigerate the cucumber mint water for at least 1 hour to allow the flavors to infuse.
- Serve chilled over ice cubes, if desired.

 Preparation Time : 5 min

 Total Time : 5 min

 Servings : 4

Nutritional Info

- Calories: 4
- Total Fat: 0g
- Cholesterol: 0mg
- Sodium: 2mg
- Total Carbohydrates: 1g
- Dietary Fiber: 0g

LEMON LIME INFUSION

Ingredients

- 1 lemon, thinly sliced
- 1 lime, thinly sliced
- Ice cubes (optional)
- Water

Instructions

- Place lemon and lime slices into a pitcher.
- Add ice cubes if desired.
- Fill the pitcher with water.
- Allow the water to infuse for at least 30 minutes before serving.
- Serve chilled and enjoy!

 Preparation Time : 5 min

 Total Time : 5 min

 Servings : 1

Nutritional Info

- Calories: 0
- Carbohydrates: 0g
- Fat: 0g
- Protein: 0g

TROPICAL FRUIT SMOOTHIE

Ingredients

- 1/2 cup frozen pineapple chunks
- 1/2 cup frozen mango chunks
- 1/2 cup frozen banana slices
- 1/2 cup coconut water
- 1/4 cup Greek yogurt
- 1 tablespoon honey (optional)
- Juice of 1/2 lime

Instructions

- Place the frozen pineapple, mango, and banana chunks in a blender.
- Add the coconut water, Greek yogurt, honey (if using), and lime juice.
- Blend on high speed until smooth and creamy, adding more coconut water if necessary to reach your desired consistency.
- Pour into a glass and serve immediately.

 Preparation Time : 5 min

 Total Time : 5 min

Servings : 1

Nutritional Info

- Calories: 150
- Protein: 3g
- Carbohydrates: 35g
- Fat: 1g
- Fiber: 5g
- Sugar: 25g

BERRY PROTEIN SHAKE

Ingredients

- 1/2 cup mixed berries (strawberries, blueberries, raspberries)
- 1/2 cup unsweetened almond milk
- 1 scoop (about 30g) vanilla protein powder
- 1/4 cup plain Greek yogurt
- 1/2 banana, frozen
- 1/2 cup ice cubes

Instructions

- Add all ingredients to a blender.
- Blend on high speed until smooth and creamy, about 1-2 minutes.
- If the shake is too thick, add more almond milk, a little at a time, until desired consistency is reached.
- Pour into a glass and enjoy immediately!

 Preparation Time : 5 min

 Total Time : 5 min

 Servings : 1

Nutritional Info

- Calories: 200 kcal
- Protein: 20g
- Carbohydrates: 25g
- Fat: 2g
- Fiber: 5g

SPICED APPLE CIDER

Ingredients

- 6 medium apples, quartered (use a mix of sweet and tart varieties)
- 1 orange, sliced
- 3 cinnamon sticks
- 1 tablespoon whole cloves
- 1 tablespoon whole allspice berries
- 1 teaspoon ground nutmeg
- 8 cups water

Instructions

- In a large pot, combine the quartered apples, orange slices, cinnamon sticks, whole cloves, whole allspice berries, ground nutmeg, and water.
- Bring the mixture to a boil over medium-high heat.
- Once boiling, reduce the heat to low and let the cider simmer for 30 minutes, uncovered, stirring occasionally.
- After 30 minutes, remove the pot from the heat and let it cool slightly.
- Using a fine mesh strainer or cheesecloth, strain the cider into a pitcher or another container to remove the solids.
- Serve the spiced apple cider warm, or refrigerate it for a few hours to serve chilled.
- Optionally, garnish each serving with a cinnamon stick or a slice of fresh apple.

 Preparation Time : 5 min

 Total Time : 35 min

Servings : 4

Nutritional Info

- Calories: 60
- Total Fat: 0g
- Saturated Fat: 0g
- Cholesterol: 0mg
- Sodium: 5mg
- Total Carbohydrates: 16g

MATCHA GREEN TEA LATTE

Ingredients

- 1 teaspoon matcha green tea powder
- 1/4 cup hot water (not boiling)
- 3/4 cup unsweetened almond milk (or any milk of choice)
- 1-2 teaspoons honey or sweetener of choice (optional)

Instructions

- Prepare Matcha: Sift 1 teaspoon of matcha green tea powder into a mug to avoid clumps.
- Add Water: Pour 1/4 cup of hot water (not boiling) into the mug with the matcha powder. Whisk vigorously using a bamboo whisk or a small regular whisk until the matcha is fully dissolved and frothy.
- Heat Milk: In a small saucepan, heat 3/4 cup of unsweetened almond milk over medium heat until it is warm but not boiling. You can also heat the milk in the microwave for about 1-2 minutes.
- Combine: Pour the heated milk into the mug with the matcha mixture. Stir to combine.
- Sweeten (Optional): If desired, add 1-2 teaspoons of honey or your preferred sweetener and stir until dissolved.
- Serve: Enjoy your Matcha Green Tea Latte immediately while warm.

 Preparation Time : 5 min

 Total Time : 10 min

 Servings : 1

Nutritional Info

- Calories: 40 (without sweetener)
- Protein: 1g
- Fat: 3g
- Carbohydrates: 2g
- Fiber: 1g
- Sugar: 0g (without sweetener)

GREEN DETOX SMOOTHIE

Ingredients

- 1 cup spinach, washed
- 1/2 cup kale, washed and stems removed
- 1/2 ripe avocado, peeled and pitted
- 1/2 banana, peeled
- 1/2 cup cucumber, peeled and chopped
- 1/2 cup unsweetened almond milk (or any milk of choice)
- Juice of 1/2 lemon
- 1 teaspoon grated ginger

Instructions

- Place all the ingredients into a blender.
- Blend on high speed until smooth and creamy.
- If the smoothie is too thick, add more almond milk to reach your desired consistency.
- Taste and adjust sweetness by adding more banana if needed.
- Pour into a glass and enjoy immediately.

 Preparation Time : 5 min

 Total Time : 5 min

 Servings : 1

Nutritional Info

- Calories: 150 kcal
- Protein: 5g
- Carbohydrates: 25g
- Fat: 3g
- Fiber: 8g

HERBAL ICED TEA

Ingredients

- 1 herbal tea bag (such as chamomile, peppermint, or hibiscus)
- 1 cup water
- Ice cubes
- Optional: sweetener of your choice (honey, stevia, agave syrup)

Instructions

- Boil 1 cup of water in a kettle or saucepan.
- Place the herbal tea bag in a heat-proof glass or mug.
- Pour the boiling water over the tea bag.
- Let the tea steep for 3-5 minutes, depending on your desired strength.
- Remove the tea bag and discard it.
- Allow the brewed tea to cool to room temperature.
- Once cooled, transfer the tea to a glass filled with ice cubes.
- Optionally, sweeten the tea with your preferred sweetener, stirring until dissolved.
- Garnish with a slice of lemon, a sprig of mint, or a slice of cucumber, if desired.
- Serve immediately and enjoy your refreshing Herbal Iced Tea!

 Preparation Time : 5 min

 Total Time : 5 min

 Servings : 1

Nutritional Info

- Calories: 0 kcal
- Carbohydrates: 0 g
- Protein: 0 g
- Fat: 0 g
- Fiber: 0 g

BERRY LEMONADE

Ingredients

- 1 cup fresh strawberries, hulled and sliced
- 1 cup fresh blueberries
- 1 cup fresh raspberries
- 1 cup fresh blackberries
- 1 cup fresh lemon juice (about 4-6 lemons)
- 4 cups cold water
- 1-2 tablespoons honey or a natural sweetener (optional)
- Ice cubes
- Fresh mint leaves for garnish (optional)

Instructions

- Wash the strawberries, blueberries, raspberries, and blackberries thoroughly.
- Hull and slice the strawberries.
- Place the strawberries, blueberries, raspberries, and blackberries in a blender.
- Blend until smooth.
- Pour the blended berry mixture through a fine mesh sieve or cheesecloth into a large pitcher to remove seeds and pulp. Use a spoon to press the mixture through the sieve if needed.
- Add the freshly squeezed lemon juice to the pitcher.
- Pour in the cold water and stir well.
- If desired, add honey or your preferred natural sweetener to the pitcher and stir until dissolved.
- Fill glasses with ice cubes.
- Pour the berry lemonade over the ice.
- Garnish with fresh mint leaves if desired.
- Serve immediately and enjoy your refreshing berry lemonade!

Preparation Time : 15 min

Total Time : 15 min

Servings : 4

Nutritional Info

- Calories: 50
- Protein: 1g
- Carbohydrates: 13g
- Dietary Fiber: 4g
- Sugars: 9g
- Fat: 0g

CONCLUSION

Thank you for embarking on this culinary journey with us through "Endomorph Diet for Women Over 60." We hope this cookbook has not only provided you with a treasure trove of delicious, nutritious recipes but also empowered you with the knowledge and tools to take control of your health and well-being.

As you turn the last page, take a moment to celebrate your commitment to a healthier lifestyle. The recipes and tips within these pages are designed to nourish your body, satisfy your taste buds, and enhance your life. Each meal you prepare and enjoy is a step toward a stronger, more vibrant you.

The endomorph diet, tailored specifically for women over 60, is more than a diet—it's a lifestyle transformation. It's about understanding your body, fueling it with the right nutrients, and embracing a balanced approach to eating that honors your unique needs. This cookbook is a roadmap to a healthier future, filled with vibrant flavors and wholesome ingredients that support your journey.

Remember, you are not alone on this journey. Join online communities, seek support from friends and family, and share your successes and challenges. The collective wisdom and encouragement of a supportive community can be a powerful motivator.

As you continue to explore and adapt these recipes to suit your tastes and lifestyle, keep experimenting and discovering new flavors. Let this cookbook be a starting point for your culinary adventures, inspiring you to create meals that are both healthy and delightful.

Here's to the new chapter you've started, one filled with delicious meals, healthier choices, and a renewed sense of well-being. May each recipe bring you joy and satisfaction, and may your journey be as rewarding as the meals you create.

Wishing you endless culinary success and a lifetime of health and happiness. Cheers to you and your vibrant future!

GLOSSARY

· · · · · · · · · ·

General Nutrition Terms

- Calories: A measure of energy provided by food.
- Macronutrients: Nutrients required in large amounts, including carbohydrates, proteins, and fats.
- Micronutrients: Essential vitamins and minerals needed in smaller amounts.
- Antioxidants: Compounds that protect cells from damage caused by free radicals.
- Fiber: A type of carbohydrate that aids digestion and is found in fruits, vegetables, and whole grains.

Diet and Health

- Endomorph: A body type characterized by a higher percentage of body fat and a tendency to gain weight easily.
- Metabolism: The process by which your body converts food into energy.
- Glycemic Index (GI): A ranking of carbohydrates based on their effect on blood glucose levels.
- Omega-3 Fatty Acids: Essential fats found in fish and some plant sources that support heart health.

Cooking and Preparation

- Al Dente: Pasta cooked to be firm to the bite.
- Blanching: Briefly boiling vegetables and then plunging them into ice water to halt the cooking process.
- Braising: Cooking food slowly in a small amount of liquid in a covered pot.
- Sautéing: Cooking food quickly in a small amount of oil over high heat.
- Steaming: Cooking food using steam, typically by placing it in a steamer basket over boiling water.

Ingredients

- Whole Grains: Grains that contain all parts of the grain kernel (bran, germ, and endosperm).
- Lean Proteins: Proteins low in fat, such as chicken breast, fish, and legumes.
- Healthy Fats: Fats from sources like avocados, nuts, and olive oil that support overall health.
- Superfoods: Nutrient-rich foods considered to be especially beneficial for health and well-being.

General Nutrition Terms

Labeling and Purchasing

- Organic: Foods produced without synthetic pesticides, fertilizers, or genetically modified organisms (GMOs).
- Non-GMO: Foods that do not contain genetically modified organisms.
- Gluten-Free: Foods that do not contain gluten, a protein found in wheat, barley, and rye.
- Low-Sodium: Foods that contain 140 mg of sodium or less per serving.

Meal Planning and Diets

- Portion Control: Managing the amount of food consumed in one sitting to maintain a balanced diet.
- Balanced Diet: A diet that includes a variety of foods in the right proportions to maintain health.
- Meal Prep: The process of preparing meals in advance to save time and ensure healthy eating habits.

Additional Terms

- Probiotics: Live beneficial bacteria found in fermented foods that support gut health.
- Prebiotics: Non-digestible food components that promote the growth of beneficial bacteria in the gut.

INDEX
. . . .

Index

Index

● ● ●

HERE IS YOUR 14 DAYS MEAL PLAN

DISCOVER MORE ABOUT MY CULINARY ADVENTURES AND UPCOMING PROJECTS.

My Weekly
Meal Planner

DAY	BREAKFAST	LUNCH	DINNER
MONDAY	Egg White Omelet with Spinach and Tomatoes	Grilled Chicken and Vegetable Salad	Baked Lemon Herb Salmon
TUESDAY	Greek Yogurt Parfait with Fresh Berries	Quinoa and Black Bean Salad	Turkey Meatballs with Zoodles
WEDNESDAY	Avocado Toast with Poached Egg	Turkey Lettuce Wraps	Veggie Stir-Fry with Tofu
THURSDAY	Banana Oat Pancakes	Zucchini Noodles with Pesto	Grilled Shrimp Skewers
FRIDAY	Smoked Salmon and Cucumber Salad	Spicy Tuna and Avocado Bowl	Herb-Crusted Chicken Breast
SATURDAY	Berry Smoothie Bowl	Chicken Caesar Salad	Balsamic Glazed Chicken Breast
SUNDAY	Egg Muffins with Veggies	Veggie and Hummus Wrap	Grilled Vegetable Kebabs

VAKARE RIMKUTE

My Weekly
Meal Planner

DAY	BREAKFAST	LUNCH	DINNER
MONDAY	Chia Seed Breakfast Pudding	Grilled Portobello Mushroom Burger	Baked Cod with Lemon and Dill
TUESDAY	Shakshuka with Fresh Herbs	Spinach and Strawberry Salad	Spaghetti Squash with Marinara Sauce
WEDNESDAY	Oatmeal with Fresh Fruit and Nuts	Cucumber & Tomato Salad with Feta	Beef and Broccoli Stir-Fry
THURSDAY	Crunchy Celery and Apple Salad	Chicken and Vegetable Soup	Roasted Chickpeas
FRIDAY	Smoked Salmon and Cucumber Salad	Lentil and Spinach Stew	Garlic and Parmesan Roasted Broccoli
SATURDAY	Marinated Mushroom Skewer	Tomato Basil Soup	Cauliflower Rice Pilaf
SUNDAY	Mango and Pineapple Salad	Seafood Chowder	Herb-Crusted Chicken Breast

VAKARE RIMKUTE

About

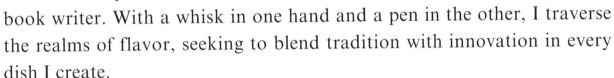

THE AUTHOR

Hello, culinary adventurers!
I'm Vakare Rimkute, a passionate explorer
of the culinary world and a devoted recipe
book writer. With a whisk in one hand and a pen in the other, I traverse
the realms of flavor, seeking to blend tradition with innovation in every
dish I create.

Growing up in the bustling kitchens of my Lithuanian grandmother, I
developed an insatiable curiosity for the alchemy of ingredients and the
magic they could weave on the palate. From the rustic charm of hearty
stews to the delicate intricacies of pastries, my journey through food has
been nothing short of a delightful adventure.

After years of experimenting and honing my craft, I found my true
calling as a recipe book writer. With each recipe I pen, I aim to capture
the essence of culinary culture while infusing it with a touch of modern
flair. From comforting classics to bold culinary experiments, my recipes
are a reflection of my belief that food should not only nourish the body
but also nourish the soul.

So join me on this gastronomic journey, where every page is filled with
tantalizing flavors, heartwarming stories, and a dash of humor.
Together, let's embark on a culinary adventure that will tickle your taste
buds and leave you craving for more. Happy cooking!

Made in United States
Troutdale, OR
12/12/2024

26382852R00062